ESSENTIAL
IDIOMS
IN
ENGLISH

NEW EDITION

ESSENTIAL IDIOMS IN ENGLISH

ROBERT J. DIXSON

PRENTICE HALL REGENTS
Englewood Cliffs, New Jersey 07632

Dixson, Robert James.
    Essential Idioms in English / Robert J. Dixson. — — New ed.
        p.   cm.
    Includes index.
    ISBN 0-13-582025-1
    1. English language— —Textbooks for foreign speakers. 2. English
  language— —Idioms. I. Title.
PE1128.D513 1994

Acquisitions editor: *Nancy Baxer*
Managing editor: *Sylvia Moore*
Editorial/production
 supervision: *Christine McLaughlin Mann*
Copyeditor: *Sandra Di Somma*
Cover designer: *Laura Ierardi*
Cover illustrator: *Merle Krumper*
Pre-press buyer: *Ray Keating*
Manufacturing buyer: *Lori Bulwin*

© 1994 R.J. Dixson Associates
Published by Prentice Hall Regents
Prentice-Hall Inc.
A Simon & Schuster Company
Englewood Cliffs, New Jersey 07632

Printed on Recycled Paper

Printed in the United States of America

10   9   8   7   6   5

ISBN   0-13-582025-1

Prentice-Hall International (UK) Limited, London
Prentice-Hall of Australia Pty. Limited, Sydney
Prentice-Hall Canada Inc., Toronto
Prentice-Hall Hispanoamericana, S.A., Mexico
Prentice-Hall of India Private Limited, New Delhi
Prentice-Hall of Japan, Inc., Tokyo
Simon & Schuster Asia Pte. Ltd., Singapore
Editora Prentice-Hall do Brasil, Ltda., *Rio de Janeiro*

Contents

Section 2   Intermediate

Section 3   Advanced   143

Foreword

Idiomatic expressions have long played an important role in the English language. In fact, the use of idioms is so widespread that an understanding of these expressions is essential to successful communication, whether in listening, speaking, reading, or writing.

The student may learn grammar and, with time, acquire adequate vocabulary, but without a working knowledge of such idioms *as above all, to get along, on the whole, to look up,* etc., even the best student's speech will remain awkward and ordinary.

Of course, the idioms selected for study should have practical value and be within the student's ability to comprehend. Such expressions as *to set the world on fire* or *to wash one's dirty laundry in public* may be very colorful, but they do little to help the student achieve fluency in English.

Teachers of English have long recognized that idiomatic expressions add grace and exactness to the language. The alert teacher will make their study an integral part of the teaching process. However, learning such expressions is never an easy task for the student learning English as a second or foreign language. Attempts to translate literally from the student's native tongue usually lead to roundabout expression of meaning and, more often, to confusion.

For this reason, only basic idioms have been included in this book, appropriately named *Essential Idioms in English, New Edition.* Furthermore, it was decided not to burden the student with discussion of the origins of idioms. There is no need to define the exact nature of an idiom except to assume that it is a phrase that has a meaning different from the meanings of its individual parts. This helps to explain why it is often difficult to translate an idiom from one language to another without incurring some change in meaning or usage.

For the purposes of this book, *two-word verbs* are included in the general category of idioms. A two-word verb is a verb whose meaning is altered by the addition of a *particle* (a preposition used with a verb to form an idiomatic expression.) *To look*, for example, may become to *look up* or *to look over,* each having its own special meaning. When a two-word verb can be separated by a noun or pronoun, the symbol (**S**) for *separable* is inserted in the definition. Sentences illustrating both separable and nonseparable forms are included in the examples.

Experienced ESL and EFL teachers will agree, for the most part, with the selection of idioms in this text. However, it should be recognized that any selection is somewhat arbitrary because the range is so great. Some teachers might prefer to omit certain idioms and to add others not included, but all should appreciate the attempt to make *Essential Idioms in English, New Edition* as representative as possible.

Mention should be made of a unique feature that adds to the usefulness of this book: Appendix II is a listing of the idioms in the text with their equivalents in Spanish, French, and German. Having these equivalents should give the student a surer grasp of the meaning of the English idioms and greater confidence in using them.

This fourth revision of *Essential Idioms in English, New Edition* has undergone several important changes. The text has been restored to the original three-section format: Elementary (lessons 1–13), Intermediate (lessons 14–27), and Advanced (lessons 28–39). As would be expected, new idioms have been included and outdated idioms have been removed. Lessons in all sections review and build upon idioms introduced in earlier lessons. In some cases, notes that explain special usage or meaning are provided after the definitions, and related idiomatic forms are listed. New types of exercises provide greater variety in activity from one section to another. Finally, there is an answer key in the back of the book for all multiple–choice, matching, true-false, and fill-in-the-blank exercises.

ESSENTIAL
IDIOMS
IN
ENGLISH

Section 1
Elementary

LESSON 1

to get in/to get on: to enter or to board a vehicle
To get in is used for cars; *to get on* is used for all other forms of transportation.

- ○ It's easiest to *get in* the car from the driver's side. The door on the other side doesn't work well.
- ○ I always *get on* the bus to work at 34th Street.

to get out of/to get off: to leave or to descend from a vehicle
To get out of is used for cars; *to get off* is used for all other forms of transportation.

- ○ Why don't we stop and *get out of* the car for a while?
- ○ Helen *got off* the train at the 42nd Street terminal.

to put on: to place on oneself (usually said of clothes) **(S)***

- ○ Mary *put on* her coat and left the room.
- ○ *Put* your hat *on* before you leave the house.

to take off: to remove (usually said of clothes) **(S)**

- ○ John *took off* his jacket as he entered the office.
- ○ *Take* your sweater *off.* The room is very warm.

to call up: to telephone (also: **to give someone a call**) **(S)**
To call can be used instead of *to call up,* as in the first example below.

- ○ I forgot to *call up* Mr. Jones yesterday. I'd better *call* him now.
- ○ *Call me up* tomorrow, Jane. We'll arrange a time to have lunch together.
- ○ I promise to *give you a call* as soon as I arrive in New York.

*The symbol (**S**) indicates that an idiom is *separable*—that a noun or noun phrase may be placed between the verb and the special preposition (called a *particle*). In these cases, examples of both separable and inseparable forms are given. See the index, page 241 for further details.

to turn on: to start or cause to function (also: **to switch on**) (S)

- ○ Please *turn on* the light; it's too dark in here.
- ○ Do you know who *turned* the air conditioning *on*?

to turn off: to cause to stop functioning (also: **to switch off, to shut off**) (S)

Turn on and *turn off,* as well as their related forms, are used for things that flow, such as electricity, water, gas, etc.

- ○ Please *turn off* the light when you leave the room.
- ○ Are you really listening to the radio, or should I *turn* it *off?*

right away: very soon; immediately (also: **at once**)

- ○ Dad says that dinner will be ready *right away*, so we'd better wash our hands and set the table.
- ○ Tell Will to come to my office *right away*. I must see him immediately.
- ○ Stop playing that loud music *at once!*

to pick up: to lift from the floor, table, etc., with one's fingers (S)

- ○ Harry *picked up* the newspaper that was on the front doorstep.
- ○ Could you *pick* your toy *up* before someone falls over it?

sooner or later: eventually, after a period of time

- ○ If you study English seriously, *sooner or later* you'll become fluent.
- ○ I'm too tired to do my homework now; I'm sure I'll do it *sooner or later.*

to get up: to arise, to rise from a bed; to make someone arise (S)

For the last definition a noun phrase must separate the verb and particle.

- ○ Carla *gets up* at seven o'clock every morning.
- ○ At what time should we *get* the children *up* tomorrow?

at first: in the beginning, originally

- ○ *At first* English was difficult for him, but later he made great progress.
- ○ I thought *at first* that it was Sheila calling, but then I realized that it was Betty.

EXERCISES

Choose the appropriate idiomatic expression to substitute for the italicized word or words in each sentence below.

1. His alarm clock is always set for six o'clock. He *arises* at the same time every day.

   a. turns off
   b. gets up
   c. puts on

2. She *telephoned* her friend to tell him about the meeting. They decided to drive there together.

   a. turned on
   b. took off
   c. called up

3. It's 4 P.M. now, and this important letter must be mailed today. Can you take it to the post office *immediately*?

   a. at first
   b. right away
   c. sooner or later

4. Be sure *to switch off* the light before you leave the house.

   a. to turn off
   b. to take off
   c. to get off

5. Pat *placed* her new hat *on her head* while looking in the mirror.

   a. picked up
   b. put on
   c. gets on

6. *Remove* your jacket and sit down for a few minutes.

   a. Turn on
   b. Get on
   c. Take off

7. I want to stay unmarried for a while, but I hope to get married *eventually*.

   a. sooner or later
   b. right away
   c. at first

8. *In the beginning* I thought that it was Bob who was in the car.

   a. To get on
   b. At once
   c. At first

9. He *boarded* the bus at Broadway and 79th Street.

   a. got off
   b. got on
   c. picked up

10. John *took* the pencil *with his fingers* and began to write a note.

    a. turned on
    b. got off
    c. picked up

Fill in each blank with the appropriate form of an idiomatic expression from this unit.

Jean's alarm clock makes a loud ringing noise. She

_____ the alarm clock immediately

after it rings each morning. However, she doesn't rise from

bed _____. She waits a few minutes

before she _____.

Jean enjoys lying in bed for a while, but

_____ she gets up. Then she

_____ the bedroom light and goes to

her closet. She _____ her pajamas and

_____ her work clothes.

L E S S O N (2)

to dress up: to wear formal clothes, to dress very nicely
- ○ We should definitely *dress up* to go to the theater.
- ○ You don't have to *dress up* for Mike's party.

at last: finally, after a long time
- ○ We waited for hours and then the train arrived *at last*.
- ○ Now that I am sixteen, *at last* I can drive my parents' car.

as usual: as is the general case, as is typical
- ○ George is late for class *as usual*. This seems to happen every day.
- ○ *As usual*, Dora received first prize in the swimming contest. It's the third consecutive year that she has won.

to find out: get information about, to determine (S)
This idiom is separable only when a pronoun is used, as in the second example.
- ○ Will you please try to *find out* what time the airplane arrives?
- ○ I'll call right now to *find it out*.

to look at: give one's attention to; to watch

- ○ The teacher told us to *look at* the blackboard and not at our books.
- ○ I like to walk along a country road at night and *look at* the stars.

to look for: to try to find, to search for
An adverb phrase such as *all over* can be put between the verb and preposition, as in the second example. However, the idiom cannot be separated by a noun or pronoun.

- ○ He's spent over an hour *looking for* the pen that he lost.
- ○ So there you are! We've *looked* all over *for* you.

all right: acceptable, fine; yes, okay
This idiom can also be spelled *alright* in informal usage.

- ○ He said that it would be *all right* to wait in her office until she returned.
- ○ Do you want me to turn off the TV? *Alright,* if you insist.

all along: all the time, from the beginning (without change)

- ○ She knew *all along* that we'd never agree with his plan.
- ○ You're smiling! Did you know *all along* that I'd give you a birthday present?

little by little: gradually, slowly (also: **step by step**)

- ○ Karen's health seems to be improving *little by little.*
- ○ If you study regularly each day, *step by step* your vocabulary will increase.

to tire out: to make very weary due to difficult conditions or hard effort (also: **to wear out**) (S)

- ○ The hot weather *tired out* the runners in the marathon.
- ○ Does studying for final exams *wear* you *out*? It makes me feel *worn out!*

to call on: to ask for a response from; to visit (also: **to drop in on**)

- ○ Jose didn't know the answer when the teacher *called on* him.
- ○ Last night several friends *called on* us at our home.
- ○ Why don't we *drop in on* Sally a little later?

never mind: don't be concerned about it; ignore what was just said

- ○ When he spilled his drink on my coat, I said, "*Never mind*. It needs to be cleaned anyway."
- ○ So you weren't listening to me again. *Never mind*; it wasn't important.

EXERCISES

Choose the appropriate idiomatic expression to substitute for the italicized word or words in each sentence below. Idioms from previous lessons are indicated by number.

1. Nan is *trying to find* the purse that she lost yesterday.
   - **a.** finding out
   - **b.** looking at
   - **c.** looking for

2. *As is typical*, Doug is late for the meeting.
   - **a.** At last
   - **b.** All along
   - **c.** As usual

3. Were you able *to determine* what his occupation is?
   - **a.** to find out
   - **b.** to pick up (Lesson 1)
   - **c.** to call on

4. I am *very weary* after all that physical exercise today.
   - **a.** turned off (Lesson 1)
   - **b.** tired out
   - **c.** never mind

5. John's mother knew that he wasn't telling the truth *from the beginning.*

 a. all along
 b. all right
 c. little by little

6. Some old friends of mine *visited* us last night.

 a. called on
 b. called up (Lesson 1)
 c. wore out

7. *Eventually,* Mario will be able to speak English better than he does now.

 a. Never mind
 b. Sooner or later (Lesson 1)
 c. At last

8. Is it *acceptable* for Mary to borrow our car for a few hours?

 a. right away (Lesson 1)
 b. all right
 c. step by step

9. Would you please *give your attention to* me while I'm talking?

 a. dress up
 b. look at
 c. wear out

10. They waited for forty-five minutes until *finally* the waiter brought their food.

 a. at last
 b. little by little
 c. at first (Lesson 1)

Fill in each blank with the appropriate form of an idiomatic expression from this unit only.

Bob: Jim, should we _____ for the

 party tonight?

Jim: No, informal clothes are fine. I'm
_____ my shoes. Have you seen
them?

Bob: No. Did you check that closet by the front door?

Jim: Of course, I did! Gosh, my legs hurt. I'm really
_____ from playing so much soccer today.

Bob: What did you say?

Jim: Oh, _____. It wasn't important.

Bob: Sorry, I'm _____ the TV news. It's
about the robbery.

Jim: Have the police _____ who stole
the million dollars?

Bob: No, they haven't.

Jim: _____ I've found my shoes! They
were in that closet by the door
_____!

Bob: I told you so!

LESSON **3**

to pick out: to choose, to select (S)

○ Ann *picked out* a good book to give to her brother as a
graduation gift.

○ Johnny, if you want me to buy you a toy, then *pick*
one *out* now.

to take one's time: to do without rush, not to hurry
This idiom is often used in the imperative form. (See the first example.)

- ○ There's no need to hurry doing those exercises. *Take your time.*
- ○ William never works rapidly. He always *takes his time* in everything that he does.

to talk over: to discuss or consider a situation with others (S)

- ○ We *talked over* Carla's plan to install an air conditioner in the room, but we couldn't reach a decision.
- ○ Before I accepted the new job offer, I *talked* the matter *over* with my wife.

to lie down: to place oneself in a flat position, to recline

- ○ If you are tired, why don't you *lie down* for an hour or so?
- ○ The doctor says that Grace must *lie down* and rest for a short time every afternoon.

to stand up: to rise from a sitting or lying position (also: **to get up**)

- ○ When the president entered the room, everyone *stood up.*
- ○ Suzy, stop rolling around on the floor; *get up* now.

to sit down: to be seated (also: **to take a seat**)

- ○ We *sat down* on the park bench and watched the children play.
- ○ There aren't any more chairs, but you can *take a seat* on the floor.

all (day, week, month, year) long: the entire day, week, month, year

- ○ I've been working on my income tax forms *all day long.* I've hardly had time to eat.
- ○ It's been raining *all week long.* We haven't seen the sun since last Monday.

by oneself: alone, without assistance

- ○ Francis translated that French novel *by himself.* No one helped him.

○ Paula likes to walk through the woods *by herself,* but her brother prefers to walk with a companion.

on purpose: for a reason, deliberately
This idiom is usually used when someone does something wrong or unfair.

○ Do you think that she didn't come to the meeting *on purpose?*

○ It was no accident that he broke my glasses. He did it *on purpose.*

to get along with: to associate or work well with; to succeed or manage in doing (also: **to get on with**)

○ Terry isn't *getting along with* her new roommate; they argue constantly.

○ How are you *getting on with* your studies?

to make a difference (to): to be of importance (to), to affect
This idiom is often used with adjectives to show the degree of importance.

○ It *makes a big difference to* me whether he likes the food I serve.

○ Does it *make any difference to* you where we go for dinner?

○ No, it doesn't *make any difference.*

○ It *makes no difference to* Lisa either.

to take out: to remove, to extract (S); to go on a date with (S) (also: **to go out with**)

○ Students, *take out* your books and open them to page twelve.

○ Did you *take* Sue *out* last night?

○ No, she couldn't *go out with* me.

EXERCISES

Choose the appropriate idiomatic expression to substitute for the italicized word or words in each sentence below. Idioms from previous lessons are indicated by number.

1. I think that you should *remove* the last two sentences in the paragraph.

    a. take out
    b. pick out
    c. talk over

2. If you *don't hurry* in completing your schoolwork, you'll do a better job.

    a. get off (Lesson 1)
    b. lie down
    c. take your time

3. How are you *succeeding in* your new job?

    a. getting on with
    b. making a difference to
    c. picking out

4. I don't like to go to the movies *alone*.

    a. as usual (Lesson 2)
    b. by myself
    c. on purpose

5. Do you have a moment *to try to find* my keys with me?

    a. to talk over
    b. to look for (Lesson 2)
    c. to get up

6. The child said that she didn't break the window *deliberately*.

    a. on purpose
    b. all day long
    c. making a difference

7. Did you *go on a date with* your new girlfriend again today?

   a. get along with
   b. stand up
   c. go out with

8. It's cold outside; you'd better *place* a sweater *on yourself.*

   a. sit down
   b. put on (Lesson 1)
   c. take out

9. Fortunately, Marie is *associating well with* her new co-workers.

   a. calling on (Lesson 2)
   b. talking over
   c. getting along with

10. Don't sit on the dirty ground like that; *rise* right now!

    a. get up
    b. lie down
    c. sit down

Fill in each blank with the appropriate form of an idiomatic expression from this unit only.

Jean: Hi, Pete. Did you come _____?

Pete: Yes, Sarah wasn't able to come. She's at the dentist's office.

Jean: Oh? Why is that?

Pete: The dentist has to _____ one of her teeth. She has been complaining of pain _____ week _____.

Jean: That's too bad. Well, I'm glad you're early.

Pete: Why? I didn't come early _____.

Jean: I know, but now we have time to _____ that important matter about the new employee.

Pete: You mean the employee who's not _____
her co-workers?

Jean: Exactly. But please, take off your coat first and
_____ on the couch.

Pete: Thanks.

L E S S O N 4

to take part in: to be involved in, to participate in (also: **to be in on**)

○ Martin was sick and could not *take part in* the meeting yesterday.

○ I didn't want to *be in on* their argument, so I remained silent.

at all: to any degree (also: **in the least**)
This idiom is used with the negative to add emphasis to a statement.

○ Larry isn't *at all* shy about expressing his opinions.

○ When I asked Donna whether she was tired, she said, "Not *in the least*. I'm full of energy."

to look up: to locate information in a directory, dictionary, book, etc. **(S)**

○ Ellen suggested that we *look up* Lee's telephone number in the directory.

○ Students should try to understand the meaning of a new word from context before *looking* the word *up* in the dictionary.

to wait on: to serve in a store or restaurant

○ A very pleasant young clerk *waited on* me in that shop.

○ The restaurant waitress asked us, "Has anyone *waited on* you yet?"

at least: a minimum of, no fewer (or less) than

- ○ I spend *at least* two hours every night on my studies.
- ○ Mike claims that he drinks *at least* a quart of water every day.

so far: until now, until the present time (also: **up to now, as of yet**)
This idiom is usually used with the present perfect tense.

- ○ *So far*, this year has been excellent for business. I hope that the good luck continues.
- ○ How many idioms have we studied in this book *up to now*?
- ○ *As of yet*, we have not had an answer from him.

to take a walk, stroll, hike, etc.: to go for a walk, stroll, hike, etc.
A *stroll* involves slow, easy walking; a *hike* involves serious, strenuous walking.

- ○ Last evening we *took a walk* around the park.
- ○ It's a fine day. Would you like to *take a stroll* along Mason Boulevard?
- ○ Let's *take a hike* up Cowles Mountain this afternoon.

to take a trip: to go on a journey, to travel

- ○ I'm so busy at work that I have no time to *take a trip*.
- ○ During the summer holidays, the Thompsons *took a trip* to Europe.

to try on: to wear clothes to check the style or fit before buying **(S)**

- ○ He *tried on* several suits before he picked out a blue one.
- ○ Why don't you *try* these shoes *on* next?

to think over: to consider carefully before deciding **(S)**

- ○ I'd like to *think over* your offer first. Then can we talk it over tomorrow?
- ○ You don't have to give me your decision now. *Think* it *over* for a while.

to take place: to occur, to happen according to plan

- ○ The regular meetings of the committee *take place* in Constitution Hall.
- ○ I thought that the celebration was *taking place* at John's house.

to put away: to remove from sight, to put in the proper place (S)

- ○ Please *put away* your papers before you open the test booklet.
- ○ John *put* the notepad *away* in his desk when he was finished with it.

Choose the appropriate idiomatic expression to substitute for the italicized word or words in each sentence below. Idioms from previous lessons are indicated by number.

1. You'll have *to locate* his number in the telephone book.
   - **a.** to think over
   - **b.** to wait on
   - **c.** to look up

2. Let's *go on a serious walk* in the mountains this weekend.
   - **a.** take a hike
   - **b.** take a trip
   - **c.** take a stroll

3. You ought to spend *a minimum of* an hour outside in the fresh air.
   - **a.** in the least
   - **b.** as usual (Lesson 2)
   - **c.** at least

4. Would you like me to help you *choose* a new dress for the dance?
   - **a.** pick out (Lesson 3)
   - **b.** try on
   - **c.** put away

5. I've always wanted *to journey* to Alaska during the summer.
   a. to take a walk
   b. to take a trip
   c. to take a stroll

6. It took a long time for the store clerk *to serve* us.
   a. to call on (Lesson 2)
   b. to take part in
   c. to wait on

7. I don't enjoy this hot, humid weather *to any degree*.
   a. at all
   b. up to now
   c. at last (Lesson 2)

8. Our guest will arrive soon; please *remove* your dirty clothes *from sight*.
   a. try on
   b. put away
   c. get off (Lesson 1)

9. I'd better *switch on* the light so that we can see better in here.
   a. be in on
   b. turn on (Lesson 1)
   c. try on

10. James didn't want *to be involved in* the preparations for the conference.
    a. to take part in
    b. to take place
    c. to try on

Fill in each blank with the appropriate form of an idiomatic expression from this unit only.

Mara: Where's the store clerk?

Ted: I don't know. It's taking him too long to

_____ us.

Mara: I don't like the service in this store

_____. I feel like leaving right

now.

Ted: Oh, no, let's not do that. How many dresses have you tried on _____?

Mara: Oh, I've tried on about eight dresses.

Ted: Well, after all that time and effort, you should buy _____ one, don't you think?

Mara: No, never mind. I'm so upset that I need to _____ outside in the fresh air.

Ted: Mara, I think that you're making the wrong decision. You should _____ it _____ first. This is really a nice dress at a great price.

Mara: Well . . . I guess a few more minutes of waiting won't make a difference.

LESSON 5

to look out: to be careful or cautious (also: **to watch out**)
Both of these idioms can occur with the preposition *for*.

- ○ *"Look out!"* Jeffrey cried as his friend almost stepped in a big hole in the ground.
- ○ *Look out for* reckless drivers whenever you cross the street.
- ○ Small children should always *watch out for* strangers offering candy.

to shake hands: to exchange greetings by clasping hands

- ○ When people meet for the first time, they usually *shake hands.*
- ○ The student warmly *shook hands* with his old professor.

to get back: to return (S)

- ○ Mr. Harris *got back* from his business trip to Chicago this morning.
- ○ Could you *get* the children *back* home by five o'clock?

to catch cold: to become sick with a cold of the nose or throat

- ○ If you go out in this rain, you will surely *catch cold*.
- ○ How did she ever *catch cold* in such warm weather?

to get over: to recover from an illness; to accept a loss or sorrow

- ○ It took me over a month *to get over* my cold, but I'm finally well now.
- ○ It seems that Mr. Mason will never *get over* the death of his wife.

to make up one's mind: to reach a decision, to decide finally

- ○ Sally is considering several colleges to attend, but she hasn't *made up her mind* yet.
- ○ When are you going to *make up your mind* about your vacation plans?

to change one's mind: to alter one's decision or opinion

- ○ We have *changed our minds* and are going to Canada instead of California this summer.
- ○ Matthew has *changed his mind* several times about buying a new car.

for the time being: temporarily (also: **for now**)

- ○ *For the time being*, Janet is working as a waitress, but she really hopes to become an actress soon.
- ○ We're living in an apartment *for now*, but soon we'll be looking for a house to buy.

for good: permanently, forever

- ○ Ruth has returned to Canada *for good*. She won't ever live in the United States again.
- ○ Are you finished with school *for good*, or will you continue your studies some day?

to call off: to cancel (S)

- ○ The referee *called off* the soccer game because of the darkness.
- ○ The president *called* the meeting *off* because she had to leave town.

to put off: to postpone (S)

- ○ Many students *put off* doing their assignments until the last minute.
- ○ Let's *put* the party *off* until next weekend, okay?

in a hurry: hurried, rushed (also: **in a rush**)

- ○ Alex seems *in a hurry;* he must be late for his train again.
- ○ She's always *in a rush* in the morning to get the kids to school.

Choose the appropriate idiomatic expression to substitute for the italicized word or words in each sentence below. Idioms from previous lessons are indicated by number.

1. Will you *return* in time for dinner or will you be home late tonight?

   a. put off
   b. get back
   c. take place (Lesson 4)

2. It took me a long time *to recover from* the sadness of losing my girlfriend.

   a. to get over
   b. to look out
   c. to change my mind

3. Do you think it's too early *to telephone* Cindy this morning?

   a. to call off
   b. to call on (Lesson 2)
   c. to call up (Lesson 1)

4. James dislikes his smoking habit so much that he wants to quit *forever*.

    a. for the time being
    b. for good
    c. in a hurry

5. At the last moment, Judy *altered her decision* about getting married so quickly.

    a. changed her mind
    b. made up her mind
    c. never mind (Lesson 2)

6. Judy wanted *to postpone* the wedding for another two or three months.

    a. to call off
    b. to put off
    c. to turn off (Lesson 1)

7. I'd like you *to remove* those toys *from sight* before they get broken.

    a. to put away
    b. to take out (Lesson 3)
    c. to look out

8. If you don't wear a sweater in this cold weather, you'll *become sick*.

    a. get over
    b. catch cold
    c. tire out (Lesson 2)

9. I still have a lot of work to do, but I feel like stopping *temporarily*.

    a. in a hurry
    b. to shake hands
    c. for now

10. If you don't *be careful*, you'll cut your hands on that sharp knife.

    a. look up (Lesson 4)
    b. watch out
    c. make up your mind

Fill in each blank with the appropriate form of an idiomatic expression from this unit only.

Todd: Mark! I was wondering when you would

_____ home!

Mark: Hi, Todd. I'm sorry, but I had a late meeting today.

Todd: Usually you leave a note in the morning when you'll be late.

Mark: I know, but I had to leave _____ to catch the bus to work. I almost missed it.

Todd: Say, what do you think? Should I go to a movie tonight with Sheila and Dick, or shouldn't I? I need to _____ soon.

Mark: What do you mean? You haven't

_____ your cold yet, have you?

Todd: No, I haven't, but I feel much better.

Mark: I think that you feel better

_____ only because you stayed home all day.

Todd: I guess you're right. Do you think that I should

_____ going with them until another time?

Mark: That would be my advice.

under the weather: not feeling well, sick

- ○ John stayed home from work because he was feeling *under the weather*.
- ○ When you catch cold, you feel *under the weather*.

to hang up: to place clothes on a hook or hanger (S); to replace the receiver on the phone at the end of a conversation (S)

- ○ Would you like me to *hang up* your coat for you in the closet?
- ○ The operator told me to *hang* the phone *up* and call the number again.

to count on: to trust someone in time of need (also: **to depend on**)

- ○ I can *count on* my parents to help me in an emergency.
- ○ Don't *depend on* Frank to lend you any money; he doesn't have any.

to make friends: to become friendly with others

- ○ Patricia is a shy girl and doesn't *make friends* easily.
- ○ During the cruise Ronald *made friends* with almost everyone on the ship.

out of order: not in working condition

- ○ The elevator was *out of order*, so we had to walk to the tenth floor of the building.
- ○ We couldn't use the soft drink machine because it was *out of order*.

to get to: to be able to do something special; to arrive at a place, such as home, work, etc. For the second definition, do not use the preposition *to* with the words *home* or *there*.

- The children *got to* stay up late and watch a good movie for the family.
- I missed the bus and couldn't *get to* the office until ten o'clock.
- When are you planning to *get home* tonight?

few and far between: not frequent, unusual, rare

- The times that our children get to stay up late are *few and far between.*
- Airplane travel is very safe because accidents are *few and far between.*

to look over: to examine, to inspect closely (also: **to go over, to read over, to check over**) (S)
Go over is different from the other forms because it is not separable.

- I want to *look* my homework *over* again before I give it to the teacher.
- The politician *went over* his speech before the important presentation.
- You should never sign any legal paper without *checking* it *over* first.

to have (time) off: to have free time, not to have to work (also: **to take time off (S)**)
The related form (S) *to take time off* is used when someone makes a decision to have free time, sometimes when others might not agree with the decision.

- Every morning the company workers *have* time *off* for a coffee break.
- Several workers *took* the afternoon *off* to go to a baseball game.

to go on: to happen; to resume, to continue (also: **to keep on**)

- Many people gathered near the accident to see what was *going on.*
- I didn't mean to interrupt you. Please *go on.*
- The speaker *kept on* talking even though most of the audience had left.

to put out: to extinguish, to cause to stop functioning **(S)**
To put out has the same meaning as *to turn off* (Lesson 1) for a light fixture.

- ○ No smoking is allowed in here. Please *put out* your cigarette.
- ○ The fire fighters worked hard to *put* the brush fire *out*.
- ○ Please *put out* the light before you leave. Okay, I'll *put* it *out*.

all of a sudden: suddenly, without warning (also: **all at once**)

- ○ *All of a sudden* Ed appeared at the door. We weren't expecting him to drop by.
- ○ *All at once* Millie got up and left the house without any explanation.

Choose the appropriate idiomatic expression to substitute for the italicized word or words in each sentence below. Idioms from previous lessons are indicated by number.

1. The businessman *inspected* the contract *carefully* before signing it.
   - **a.** looked over
   - **b.** looked out (Lesson 5)
   - **c.** counted on

2. What's *happening*, John? The smoke alarm is ringing but there's no fire!
   - **a.** putting out
   - **b.** going on
   - **c.** hanging up

3. The dark clouds rolled in quickly and it began to rain *without warning*.
   - **a.** all along (Lesson 2)
   - **b.** out of order
   - **c.** all of a sudden

4. When do you think that we'll *arrive at* the hotel this evening?

   a. get on (Lesson 1)
   b. go on
   c. get to

5. I'm busy this week, but I hope *to have time free* next week.

   a. to take my time (Lesson 3)
   b. to have time off
   c. to check over

6. *Gradually* I'm learning how to play tennis, thanks to my kind instructor.

   a. Little by little (Lesson 2)
   b. All at once
   c. Few and far between

7. It's nice to know that I can *trust* you to help me when I need it.

   a. count on
   b. check over
   c. make friends

8. The phone is making noise because you forgot *to replace* the receiver.

   a. to go over
   b. to take place (Lesson 4)
   c. to hang up

9. He's so careful when he plays sports that injuries are *unusual* for him.

   a. under the weather
   b. few and far between
   c. out of order

10. The students were happy because they *were able to* leave class early.

    a. took time off to
    b. went on
    c. got to

Fill in each blank with the appropriate form of an idiomatic expression from this unit only.

Tina: What's wrong, Matt? You look _____.

Matt: I know. I don't feel well.

Tina: You looked fine an hour ago. It must have happened

_____.

Matt: It did. I was talking to Mike on the phone, and after I

_____ the receiver, it hit me.

Tina: Wow. Do you think that you can still

_____ my paper for me later?

You're good at finding my mistakes.

Matt: Of course, Tina. You can _____

me to do that for you. First, though, I'd like to lie

down.

Tina: Okay. Would you like me to _____

the light?

Matt: Thanks. I'll be fine in a while.

LESSON 7

to point out: to show, to indicate, to bring to one's attention (S)

○ What important buildings did the tour guide *point out* to you?

○ The teacher *pointed out* the mistakes in my composition.

○ A friend *pointed* the famous actor *out* to me.

to be up: to expire, to be finished

This idiom is used only with the word *time* as the subject.

- ○ "The time *is up*," the teacher said at the end of the test period.
- ○ We have to leave the tennis court because our hour *is up*; some other people want to use it now.

to be over: to be finished, to end (also: **to be through**)

This idiom is used for activities and events.

- ○ After the dance *was over*, we all went to a restaurant.
- ○ The meeting *was through* ten minutes earlier than everyone expected.

on time: exactly at the correct time, punctually

- ○ I thought that Margaret would arrive late, but she was right *on time*.
- ○ Did you get to work *on time* this morning, or did rush hour traffic delay you?

in time to: before the time necessary to do something

- ○ We entered the theater just *in time to* see the beginning of the movie.
- ○ The truck was not able to stop *in time to* prevent an accident.

to get better, worse, etc.: to become better, worse, etc.

- ○ Heather has been sick for a month, but now she is *getting better*.
- ○ This medicine isn't helping me. Instead of getting better, I'm *getting worse*.

to get sick, well, tired, busy, wet, etc.: to become sick, well, tired, busy, wet, etc.

This idiom consists of a combination of *get* and various adjectives.

- ○ Gerald *got sick* last week and has been in bed since that time.
- ○ Every afternoon I *get* very *hungry*, so I eat a snack.

had better: should, ought to, be advisable to
This idiom is most often used in contracted form (*I'd better*).

- ○ I think *you'd better* speak to Mr. White right away about this matter.
- ○ The doctor told the patient that *he'd better* go home and rest.

would rather: prefer to (also: **would just as soon**)

- ○ *Would* you *rather* have the appointment this Friday or next Monday?
- ○ I *would just as soon* go for a walk as watch TV right now.

to call it a day/night: to stop working for the rest of the day/night

- ○ Herb tried to repair his car engine all morning before he *called it a day* and went fishing.
- ○ We've been working hard on this project all evening; let's *call it a night.*

to figure out: to solve, to find a solution (S); to understand (S)

- ○ How long did it take you *to figure out* the answer to the math problem?
- ○ I was never able *to figure* it *out.*

to think of: to have a (good or bad) opinion of
This idiom is often used in the negative or with adjectives such as *much* and *highly.*

- ○ I don't *think* much *of* him as a baseball player; he's a slow runner and a poor hitter.
- ○ James *thinks* highly *of* his new boss, who is a kind and helpful person.

Choose the appropriate idiomatic expression to substitute for the italicized word or words in each sentence below. Idioms from previous lessons are indicated by number.

1. We *were able to* visit the zoo when the animals were very active.

   a. would rather
   b. had better
   c. got to (Lesson 6)

2. All of this work in the garden has tired me out; let's *stop working.*

   a. be over
   b. call it a day
   c. be up

3. I can't *understand* Professor Jones at all; he's a very good teacher, but sometimes he talks foolishly.

   a. figure out
   b. make up my mind about (Lesson 5)
   c. point out

4. I *prefer to* eat in tonight than to eat out; what do you think?

   a. would rather
   b. had better
   c. so far (Lesson 4)

5. The police officer put a parking ticket on the car because the time on the meter *had expired.*

   a. was over
   b. was not on time
   c. was up

6. I don't *have a good opinion of* our new neighbors; they're not very friendly.

   a. make friends with (Lesson 6)
   b. get better with
   c. think much of

7. This problem is too difficult for me *to solve* by myself.
   a. to point out
   b. to be over
   c. to figure out

8. We were late to the party, but we got there *before the time* to eat dinner.
   a. to wait on
   b. in time to
   c. on time

9. Jan couldn't wait for the meeting *to end* so that she could go home.
   a. to call off (Lesson 5)
   b. to be through
   c. to get worse

10. It was supposed to be a surprise, but Larry knew about the birthday party *from the beginning.*
    a. all along (Lesson 2)
    b. on time
    c. to call it a night

Fill in each blank with the appropriate form of an idiomatic expression from this unit only.

Sue: Kay, if we're going to get to a movie _____ find good seats, we _____ hurry to decide what to see.

Kay: But we can't agree on the two possibilities!

Sue: I know. I want to see the old Humphrey Bogart film, but you _____ see the movie with the famous actor Guy Matson in it.

Kay: I can't _____ your taste in men, Sue. All the women that I know just love Guy Matson!

Sue: Kay, let me _____ again that I'm not a typical American woman. My mother is German, you know.

Kay: You like to remind me of that, don't you! Anyway, I
don't _____ much _____ old movies,
so forget about Humphrey Bogart.

Sue: Okay, okay! Let's go down to the car and make up our
minds while driving.

Kay: Good idea!

LESSON 8

to be about to: to be at the moment of doing something, to
be ready
This idiom is often used with the adverb *just*.

- I *was just about to* leave when you telephoned.
- Oh, hi, John. We're *just about to* eat dinner.

to turn around: to move or face in the opposite direction
(**S**); to completely change the condition of (**S**)

- The man *turned* his car *around* and drove back the
way he came.
- The company has been very successful since the new
business manager was able to *turn* it *around*.

to take turns: to alternate, to change people while doing
something

- During the trip, Darlene and I *took turns* driving so
that neither of us would tire out.
- I have to make sure that my two sons *take turns* playing the video game.

to pay attention (to): to look at and listen to someone while
they are speaking, to concentrate

- Please *pay attention to* me while I'm speaking to you!
- You'll have to *pay* more *attention* in class if you want
to get a good grade.

to brush up on: to review something in order to refresh one's memory

- ○ Before I travelled to Mexico, I *brushed up on* my Spanish; I haven't practiced it since high school.
- ○ In order to take that advanced mathematics class, Sidney will have to *brush up on* his algebra.

over and over (again): repeatedly (also: **time after time, time and again**)

- ○ The actress studied her lines in the movie *over and over* until she knew them well.
- ○ Children have difficulty remembering rules, so it's often necessary to repeat them *over and over again*.
- ○ *Time and again* I have to remind Bobby to put on his seatbelt in the car.

to wear out: to use something until it has no value or worth anymore, to make useless through wear (**S**)

- ○ When I *wear out* these shoes, I'll have to buy some that last longer.
- ○ What do you do with your clothes after you *wear* them *out*?

to throw away: to discard, to dispose of (**S**)

- ○ I generally *throw away* my clothes when I wear them out.
- ○ Don't *throw* the magazines *away*; I haven't read them yet.

to fall in love: to begin to love
This idiom is used with the expression *at first sight* to indicate a sudden interest in love.

- ○ Ben and Sal *fell in love* in high school, and got married after graduation.
- ○ Have you ever *fallen in love at first sight*?

to go out: to stop functioning; to stop burning; to leave home or work (also: **to step out**)

- ○ The lights *went out* all over the city because of an electrical problem.
- ○ The campers didn't have to put out the fire because it *went out* by itself.
- ○ Gary isn't here right now; he *went out* to the store for a moment.
- ○ I have to *step out* of the office briefly to pick up a newspaper.

out of the question: impossible, not feasible

- ○ Stephen told Deborah that it was *out of the question* for her to borrow his new car.
- ○ Don't expect me to do that again. It's absolutely *out of the question.*

to have to do with: to have some connection with or relationship to

- ○ Ralph insisted that he had *nothing to do with* breaking the window.
- ○ What does your suggestion *have to do with* our problem?

EXERCISES

Choose the appropriate idiomatic expression to substitute for the italicized word or words in each sentence below. Idioms from previous lessons are indicated by number.

1. Don't *discard* those old cardboard boxes; Jim can use them for packing his things when he moves to a new apartment.

   a. put away (Lesson 4)
   b. throw away
   c. wear out

2. If you had *concentrated on* what I said, I wouldn't have to repeat myself.

    a. paid attention to
    b. had to do with
    c. turned around

3. I plan to stay in school *temporarily* and take more coursework.

    a. out of the question
    b. over and over again
    c. for the time being (Lesson 5)

4. How do our children *make* their pants *useless* in such a short time?

    a. take turns
    b. dress up (Lesson 2)
    c. wear out

5. Before George takes a college-level biology class, he should *review* his biology from high school.

    a. brush up on
    b. look over (Lesson 6)
    c. be about to

6. I liked that movie so much that I could watch it *repeatedly*.

    a. out of the question
    b. taking turns
    c. over and over again

7. Betty can't *understand* why she's having trouble with the engine of her car.

    a. turn around
    b. figure out (Lesson 7)
    c. step out

8. This message from Tom *has no connection with* plans for the party tonight.

    a. is out of the question
    b. doesn't fall in love with
    c. has nothing to do with

9. Sally *was ready to* take a shower when the phone rang, so she answered it.

   a. was about to
   b. took turns to
   c. had better (Lesson 7)

10. I'm tired of working; let's *leave home* for a while and shop for groceries.

    a. turn around
    b. go out
    c. call it a day (Lesson 7)

Fill in each blank with the appropriate form of an idiomatic expression from this unit only.

Lee: Jan, you've _____ these shoes completely. Why do you keep them?

Jan: Don't ask me again, Lee! I've told you

_____—they are my favorite pair.

Lee: I know, I know. Every time we

_____ somewhere, you wear them.

Jan: It's terrible, isn't it? I know that I should

_____ such bad-looking shoes, but they're so comfortable, I can't!

Lee: What if I said that I would buy a new pair for you— would you discard them then?

Jan: That's completely _____! This situation doesn't _____ money; it's connected to my feeling for the shoes.

Lee: Feeling for the shoes! Is it possible that you have

_____ with them?

Jan: Yes, I guess I love them more than I love you!

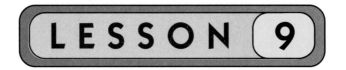

L E S S O N 9

to wake up: to arise from sleep, to awaken (S)
Compare *wake up* and *get up* (Lesson 1) as used in the first example.

- ○ Marge woke up this morning very early, but she did not *get up* until about ten o'clock.
- ○ My alarm clock *wakes* me *up* at the same time every day.

to be in charge of: to manage, to have responsibility for

- ○ Jane *is in charge of* the office while Mrs. Haig is on a business trip.
- ○ Who *is in charge of* arrangements for the dance next week?

as soon as: just after, when

- ○ *As soon as* it started to snow, the children ran outside with big smiles on their faces.
- ○ I'm busy now, but I'll meet you *as soon as* I've finished this work.

to get in touch with: to communicate with, to contact

- ○ You can *get in touch* with him by calling the Burma Hotel.
- ○ I've been trying all morning *to get in touch with* Miss Peters, but her phone is always busy.

to have a good time: to enjoy oneself

- ○ We all *had a good time* at the class reunion last night.
- ○ Did you *have a good time* at the park? I really enjoyed it.

in no time: very quickly, rapidly
This idiom can be used with the idiom *at all* to add emphasis to the certainty of the statement.

- ○ Mac said that he'd be ready to leave *in no time*.
- ○ We thought that the meeting would take two hours, but it was over *in no time at all*.

to cut down on: to reduce, to lessen (also: **to cut back on**)

- ○ In order to lose weight, you have *to cut down on* your intake of sugar.
- ○ The doctor told me *to cut back on* exercise until my back injury heals.

quite a few: many

- ○ *Quite a few* students were absent yesterday; in fact, more than half of them were not there.
- ○ We did not expect many people to attend the affair, but *quite a few* of our friends actually came.

used to: formerly did, had the habit of
This idiom is used to indicate a past situation, action, or habit that does not exist in the present. The idiom is always followed by a simple verb form.

- ○ I *used to* live in New York, but I moved to California two years ago.
- ○ Kim *used to* smoke cigarettes, but she stopped the habit last month.

to be used to: be accustomed to
This idiom refers to a situation, action, or habit that continues in the present. The idiom is always followed by a noun or gerund phrase.

- ○ He *is used to* this climate now, so the changes in temperature do not affect him much.
- ○ I *am used to* studying in the library, so it's difficult for me to study at home now.

to get used to: to become used to, to become adjusted to
This idiom describes the process of change that allows someone to be used to a situation, action, or habit.

- ○ It took Yoshiko a long time *to get used to* the food that her American host family served her.

○ Mark can't seem *to get used to* wearing contact lenses; recently he's been wearing his glasses a lot.

back and forth: in a backward and forward motion

○ The restless lion kept pacing *back and forth* along the front of its cage.

○ Grandmother finds it relaxing to sit in her rocking chair and move *back and forth*.

Choose the appropriate idiomatic expression to substitute for the italicized word or words in each sentence below. Idioms from previous lessons are indicated by number.

1. When we finally decided to eat out, we got ready *rapidly*.

   a. in no time
   b. on time (Lesson 7)
   c. as soon as

2. Joe has never been able *to become adjusted to* getting up early in the morning.

   a. used to
   b. to be used to
   c. to get used to

3. I have a lot of trouble breathing well when I run, so I guess that I should *reduce* smoking.

   a. be in charge of
   b. throw away (Lesson 8)
   c. cut down on

4. While I was reading in bed last night, the phone in the kitchen rang, so I had *to arise* to answer it.

   a. to wake up
   b. to get up (Lesson 1)
   c. to be used to

5. *Many* people at the beach were wearing jackets because the wind was cool.

   a. Quite a few
   b. As soon as
   c. Few and far between (Lesson 6)

6. Would you *contact* the Jacksons and tell them that we've put off the garage sale?

   a. get in touch with
   b. be in charge of
   c. have a good time

7. *When* my parents were ready to leave, we went out to dinner.

   a. At first (Lesson 1)
   b. As soon as
   c. All of a sudden (Lesson 6)

8. Jack *made* the engine of his car *useless* by forgetting to add oil to it regularly.

   a. got worse (Lesson 7)
   b. used to
   c. wore out (Lesson 8)

9. The boat was moving *in backward and forward motion* because of the large waves on the ocean.

   a. at least (Lesson 4)
   b. back and forth
   c. on purpose (Lesson 3)

10. Vera *had the habit to* bite her nails until they were very short, but now she's stopped doing that.

    a. has been used to
    b. used to
    c. cut back on

Fill in each blank with the appropriate form of an idiomatic expression from this unit only.

Abe: Zeke! It's already 8 A. M. It's time for you to

_____.

Zeke: What do you mean? It's the weekend, and I
_____ sleeping until at least 10
A. M. on Saturdays!

Abe: Don't you remember? We're organizing a beach picnic for our sports club today.

Zeke: Oh, I forgot about that. Just give me fifteen more minutes. I can be ready _____.

Abe: Look, there's a lot to take to the beach and to set up, like the volleyball net. We need to do it together.

Zeke: Can't you _____ the other students and tell them that the picnic will start later?

Abe: Zeke, I can't call everybody.
_____ people are planning to come.

Zeke: Boy, why did you agree that we would
_____ the picnic? It's too much responsibility.

Abe: I didn't agree. You did!

L E S S O N 10

to make sure: to be sure, to ascertain (also: **to make certain**)

○ Please *make sure* that you turn off the radio before you go out.
○ Could you *make certain* of the time? I don't want to miss that TV show.

now and then: occasionally, sometimes (also: **now and again, at times, from time to time, off and on, once in a while**)

Both *now and then* and *once in a while* can be preceded by the adjective *every*. Another idiom with the same meaning and form is *every so often*.

- ○ I don't see him very often, but (*every*) *now and then* we arrange to have lunch together.
- ○ Gary gets a cold (*every*) *once in a while* even though he takes good care of himself.
- ○ *Every so often* my brother and I get together for a camping trip.
- ○ I like to sleep late in the morning *from time to time*.

to get rid of: to eliminate, to remove; to discard, to throw away

- ○ Jerry tried hard to *get rid of* the stain on his shirt, but he never succeeded.
- ○ The stain was so bad that Jerry finally had to *get rid of* his shirt.

every other (one): every second (one), alternate (ones)

- ○ I play tennis with my father *every other* Saturday, so I usually play twice a month.
- ○ There were twenty problems in the exercise, but the teacher told us only to do *every other* one. Actually, doing ten problems was difficult enough.

to go with: to match, to compare well in color or design; to date, to accompany (also: **to go out with**)

For the first definition, adverbs such as *well* and *poorly* are often used.

- ○ That striped shirt *goes* well *with* the gray pants, but the pants *go* poorly *with* those leather shoes.
- ○ Eda *went with* Richard for about six months, but now she *is going out with* a new boyfriend.

first-rate: excellent, superb

- ○ The food served in that four-star restaurant is truly *first-rate*.

○ The Beverly Hills Hotel provides *first-rate* service to its guests.

to come from: to originate from
This idiom is commonly used in discussion of one's home-town, state, or country.

○ What country in South America does she *come from*? She *comes from* Peru.
○ I just learned that he really *comes from* Florida, not Texas.
○ Where did this package *come from*? The mail carrier brought it.

to make good time: to travel a sufficient distance at a reasonable speed
The adjective *excellent* can also be used.

○ On our last trip, it rained the entire time, so we didn't *make good time*.
○ We *made excellent time* on our trip to Florida; it only took eighteen hours.

to mix up: to stir or shake well (**S**); to confuse, to bewilder (**S**)
For the second definition, the passive forms *to be mixed up* or *to get mixed up* are often used.

○ You should *mix up* the ingredients well before you put them in the pan.
○ The teacher's poor explanation really *mixed* the students *up*.
○ The students think it's their fault that they *are mixed up* so often.

to see about: to give attention or time to (also: **to attend to, to see to**)

○ Who is going to *see about* getting us a larger room for the meeting?
○ I'll *see to* arranging music for the wedding if you *attend to* the entertainment.

to make out: to do, to succeed, to progress

- ○ Charlie didn't *make out* very well on his final examinations. He may have to repeat one or more classes.
- ○ How did Rachelle *make out* on her acting audition in Hollywood yesterday?

by heart: by memorizing

- ○ He knows many passages from Shakespeare *by heart*.
- ○ Do you know all the idioms you have studied in this book *by heart*?

E X E R C I S E S

Choose the appropriate idiomatic expression to substitute for the italicized word or words in each sentence below. Idioms from previous lessons are indicated by number.

1. Jack has been too busy with his work *to date* anyone recently.
   - **a.** to see about
   - **b.** to make out
   - **c.** to go out with

2. The manager wanted her assistant *to ascertain* when the products would be delivered.
   - **a.** to make good time
   - **b.** to get rid of
   - **c.** to make sure

3. You should *stir* the milk and eggs before you add the butter.
   - **a.** cut down on (Lesson 9)
   - **b.** mix up
   - **c.** come from

4. I was so nervous about giving the speech that I learned every word *by memorizing*.
   - **a.** by myself (Lesson 3)
   - **b.** by heart
   - **c.** now and then

5. The weather is so bad today that we should definitely *postpone* the picnic.

    a. put off (Lesson 5)
    b. call off (Lesson 5)
    c. see about

6. George never seems to study. How is he *progressing* in his coursework?

    a. making out
    b. coming from
    c. looking over (Lesson 6)

7. The test instructions were so poorly written that the students *were confused* about what to do.

    a. were attended to
    b. paid attention (Lesson 8)
    c. were mixed up

8. This yellow tie doesn't *match* your blue jacket at all.

    a. go with
    b. get rid of
    c. come from

9. John enjoys going hiking with his friends. They take a hike together *every second* weekend.

    a. every now and then
    b. every other
    c. all weekend long (Lesson 3)

10. This tablecloth is too old to use anymore; would you mind if we *discard* it?

    a. get rid of
    b. come from
    c. see to

Fill in each blank with the appropriate form of an idiomatic expression from this unit only.

Jean: Hi, Helen. I really like your blouse. It

_____ your blouse.

Helen: Thanks, Jean, but haven't you seen it before? I've had it for years, and I was planning to _____ it!

Jean: Oh, no, it still looks fine. Tell me, how are you _____ with your final class presentation? Are you still writing it?

Helen: I'm all finished. Tomorrow I'm going to practice until I know it _____.

Jean: Why don't you practice in front of me right now?

Helen: Maybe later. Right now I'd like to _____ having dinner. I'm really hungry.

Jean: Do you want to cook here, or eat out?

Helen: Let's eat out. I just heard about a new Italian restaurant that is supposed to be _____.

Jean: Sounds great. But it's almost 9 P.M.. When does it close?

Helen: I think that Jim said 9:30. It's easy to _____ on city streets at night, so I'm sure we can get there in time.

Jean: Let's go!

LESSON 11

to keep out: not to enter, not allow to enter (S)

- There was a large sign outside the door that said, "Danger! *Keep out!*"
- I've told you to *keep* the dog *out* of the house.

to keep away (from): to stay at a distance (from) (S); to avoid use of (also: **stay away from**)

- Please be sure to *keep* the children *away from* the street!
- The signs on the burned-out house said, "*Keep Away! Danger Zone.*"
- It's important for your health to *stay away from* dangerous drugs.

to find fault with: to criticize, to complain about something

- It is very easy *to find fault with* the work of others, but more difficult to accept criticism of one's own work.
- Mrs. Johnson is always *finding fault with* her children, but they really try to please their mother.

to be up to: to be responsible for deciding; to be doing as a regular activity
The second definition is most often used in a question as a form of greeting.

- I don't care whether we go to the reception or not. It's *up to* you.
- Hi, George. I haven't seen you in a while. What have you *been up to?*

ill at ease: uncomfortable or worried in a situation

- Speaking in front of a large audience makes many people feel *ill at ease.*
- My wife and I were *ill at ease* because our daughter was late coming home from a date.

to do over: to revise, to do again (S)
A noun or pronoun must separate the two parts of this idiom.

- You'd better *do* the letter *over* because it is written so poorly.
- Jose made so many mistakes in his homework that the teacher made him *do* it *over.*

to look into: to investigate, to examine carefully (also: **to check into**)

- ○ The police *are looking into* the matter of the stolen computers.
- ○ The congressional committee will *check into* the financial dealings of the government contractor.

to take hold of: to grasp, to grip with the hands

- ○ You should *take hold of* the railing as you go down those steep stairs.
- ○ The blind man *took hold of* my arm as I led him across the street.

to get through: to finish, to complete
This idiom is followed either by the *-ing* form of a verb (a gerund) or by the preposition *with*.

- ○ I didn't *get through* studying last night until almost eleven o'clock.
- ○ At what time does your wife *get through with* work every day?

from now on: from this time into the future

- ○ Mr. Lee's doctor told him to cut down on eating fatty foods *from now on*, or else he might suffer heart disease.
- ○ I'm sorry that I dropped by at a bad time. *From now on* I'll call you first.

to keep track of: to keep or maintain a record of; to remember the location of

- ○ Steve *keeps track of* all the long-distance telephone calls related to his business that he makes from his house.
- ○ With seven small children, how do the Wilsons *keep track of* all of them?

to be carried away: to be greatly affected by a strong feeling (S)
This idiom can also be used with *get* instead of *be*.

- ○ Paula and Leanne *were carried away* by the sad movie that they saw together.
- ○ James *got carried away* with anger when his roommate crashed his new car into a telephone pole.

Choose the appropriate idiomatic expression to substitute for the italicized word or words in each sentence below. Idioms from previous lessons are indicated by number.

1. It's difficult for old people *to remember the location of* personal possessions such as keys.

   a. to keep track of
   b. to keep away from
   c. to take hold of

2. I haven't seen Jackie in a long time. I wonder what she *has been doing.*

   a. has gotten through
   b. has to do with (Lesson 8)
   c. has been up to

3. Jeff agreed *to give attention to* organizing the beach barbecue this weekend.

   a. to look into
   b. to see about (Lesson 10)
   c. to do over

4. The unfriendly man told the neighborhood boys, "I don't want any of you coming in my yard. *Don't enter!*"

   a. Keep out!
   b. Be carried away!
   c. Put out! (Lesson 6)

5. Janice felt *uncomfortable* at the party because she didn't know anyone there; they were all complete strangers to her.

   a. mixed up (Lesson 10)
   b. ill at ease
   c. out of the question (Lesson 8)

6. To open the door, you have *to grasp* it firmly and pull hard.

   a. to take hold of
   b. to get through
   c. to find fault with

7. *Until now* I haven't broken any bones in my body. Knock on wood!

   a. At last (Lesson 2)
   b. From now on
   c. So far (Lesson 4)

8. Lita made so many mistakes in her essay that the teacher told her *to revise it*.

   a. to find fault with it
   b. to do it over
   c. to check into it

9. I *was greatly affected by emotion* when my friends surprised me with a big birthday celebration.

   a. was carried away
   b. was up to me
   c. had a good time (Lesson 9)

10. Mr. Smith asked the police *to investigate* the theft of his car radio last week.

    a. to look for (Lesson 2)
    b. to look over (Lesson 6)
    c. to look into

Fill in each blank with the appropriate form of an idiomatic expression from this unit only.

Max: Jeff, are you still busy?

Jeff: Of course I am! Didn't you see the sign on my door. It says, "_____!"

Max: Come on, Jeff. Give me five minutes of your time, okay?

Jeff: Okay, what is it?

Max: I just wanted to know when you're going to

_____ with your work.

Jeff: I need at least another five hours. The professor found

so many mistakes in my research paper that I have to

_____ it _____.

Max: Oh, I didn't realize that.

Jeff: I know one thing—I'm going to start all my work

much earlier and do it more carefully

_____.

Max: That's a good idea. Say, would you like a beer to

relax?

Jeff: Are you kidding? I have to _____ alco-

hol if I'm going to finish this work.

Max: Well, it's _____ you. I can write

more easily after a beer or two. Say, would you like

me to read what you've done so far?

Jeff: No way. I know what will happen—you'll just

_____ it.

Max: Okay, then. I'll just go away and leave you alone.

Jeff: Thanks, Max. Sorry I'm acting so

_____, but I need to get this done by

tomorrow. There isn't much time left.

Max: I understand. Just don't _____

and be angry at your friends!

up to date: modern; current, timely
Hyphens (-) separate the parts of this idiom when it precedes
a noun form, as in the third example. The verb *to update*
derives from this idiom.

- ○ The president insisted that the company bring its
aging equipment *up to date*.
- ○ This catalog is not *up to date*. It was published several
years ago.
- ○ The news program gave an *up-to-date* account of the
nuclear accident. The newscaster said that he would
update the news report every half hour.

out of date: not modern; not current, not timely; no longer
available in published form
Again, hyphens separate the parts of this idiom when it precedes a noun form as, in the second example. The passive
verb *to be outdated* derives from this idiom.

- ○ Many people buy new cars when their old cars
become *out of date*.
- ○ I don't know why Gene likes to wear *out-of-date* clothing. His clothes are so *outdated* that even his girlfriend
hesitates to be seen with him.
- ○ This book can't be ordered any more because it is *out
of date*.

to blow up: to inflate, to fill with air (**S**); to explode, to
destroy (or be destroyed) by explosion (**S**)

- ○ Daddy, could you please *blow up* this balloon for me?
- ○ When the airplane crashed into the ground, it *blew up*
immediately.
- ○ The military had to *blow* the missile *up* in midair
when it started to go the wrong way.

to catch fire: to begin to burn

- ○ Don't stand too close to the gas stove. Your clothes may *catch fire.*
- ○ No one seems to know how the old building *caught fire.*

to burn down: to burn slowly, but completely (usually said of candles); to destroy completely by fire (**S**)

- ○ There was a large amount of wax on the table where the candles had *burned down.*
- ○ The fire spread so quickly that the firefighters could not prevent the whole block of buildings from *burning down.*

to burn up: to destroy completely by fire (**S**); to make angry or very annoyed (**S**) (also: **to tick off**)
To burn up and *to burn down* (previous idiom) share the same definition but also have different definitions.

- ○ She didn't want anyone to see the letter, so she *burned it up* and threw the ashes away.
- ○ It really *burns* me *up* that he borrowed my car without asking me first.
- ○ Mike got *ticked off* that his friends never offered to help him move to his new apartment. He had to do everything himself.

to burn out: to stop functioning because of overuse; to make tired from too much work (**S**)

- ○ This light bulb has *burned out.* Could you get another one?
- ○ Studying all day for my final exams has really *burned* me *out.*

to make good: to succeed

- ○ He is a hard worker, and I'm sure that he *will make good* in that new job.
- ○ Alma has always *made good* in everything that she has done.

stands to reason: to be clear and logical

This idiom is almost always used with the pronoun subject *it* and is followed by a *that* clause.

- ○ *It stands to reason that* a person without experience cannot do the work as well as an experienced one.
- ○ *It stands to reason that* he isn't going to pass the course if he never studies.

to break out: to become widespread suddenly

- ○ An epidemic of measles *broke out* in Chicago this past week.
- ○ If a nuclear war ever *breaks out*, it is unlikely that many people will survive.
- ○ The news says that a large fire has *broken out* in a huge chemical plant.

as for: regarding, concerning (also: **as to**)

- ○ *As for* the money, we will simply have to borrow some more from the bank.
- ○ There is no doubt *as to* her intelligence; she's the smartest one in the class.

to feel sorry for: to pity, to feel compassion for (also: **to take pity on**)

- ○ Don't you *feel sorry for* someone who has to work the night shift?
- ○ I helped drive Pierre around when he broke his foot because I *took pity on* him.

EXERCISES

Choose the appropriate idiomatic expression to substitute for the italicized word or words in each sentence below. Idioms from previous lessons are indicated by number.

1. I had to use a lot of paper and matches before I was able to get the wood in the fireplace *to begin to burn*.

   a. to burn down

    b. to catch fire

    c. to burn up

2. If you stay up late every night, it *seems logical* that you'll get sick.

    a. stands to reason

    b. makes good

    c. feels sorry for

3. The coach *inflated* several of the players' soccer balls that were too soft.

    a. broke out

    b. made out (Lesson 10)

    c. blew up

4. *From the beginning* I knew that I wanted to go to medical school and to become a doctor.

    a. All along (Lesson 2)

    b. As for

    c. At least (Lesson 4)

5. This set of reference books is so old that the library should buy one that is more *current*.

    a. out of date

    b. first-rate (Lesson 10)

    c. up to date

6. I *pity* Marilyn because everything of value in her house was stolen by thieves.

    a. tick off

    b. count on (Lesson 6)

    c. feel sorry for

7. If you continue without taking a break, this difficult work will *make you tired*.

    a. burn you out

    b. burn you up

    c. burn you down

8. Those two sisters look so much alike that I often get *confused* about their names.

    a. mixed up (Lesson 10)

    b. broken out

    c. out of date

9. *Regarding* me, I don't care where we go today. It's up to you.
   a. To be about to (Lesson 8)
   b. As for
   c. To think of (Lesson 7)

10. It *makes me annoyed* that Jocelyn didn't call to cancel our appointment.
   a. burns me up
   b. breaks me out
   c. burns me down

Fill in each blank with the appropriate form of an idiomatic expression from this unit only.

Matt: Have you heard the news? A big fire

_____ in the downtown area

early this morning. A whole block was affected.

Lisa: Really? How many buildings have _____?

Matt: More than ten, I believe. Haven't you seen the smoke

in the air?

Lisa: Yes, I wondered what that was. Doesn't the fire

department have the fire under control by now?

Matt: No, it doesn't. Their equipment is so _____

that it isn't effective in fighting the fire.

Lisa: Boy, I bet that the people who lost their stores are really

_____ about that. I would be very

angry if it was my business.

Matt: _____ me, I _____ all the

workers who have lost their jobs because of the fire.

Lisa: It _____ that the city government is

going to have to buy _____ equipment

now.

Matt: Let's hope so.

to break down: to stop functioning

Compare this idiom with *to burn out* in Lesson 12. *To burn out* means that electrical equipment becomes hot from overuse and stops functioning. *To break down* means that something stops functioning mechanically, whether from overuse or not.

- ○ I just bought my new car yesterday and already it has *broken down.*
- ○ The elevator *broke down*, so we walked all the way up to the top floor.

to turn out: to become or result; to appear, to attend (also: **to come out**)

The noun form **turnout** derives from the second definition of the idiom.

- ○ Most parents wonder how their children will *turn out* as adults.
- ○ Hundreds of people *came out* for the demonstration against new taxes.
- ○ What was the *turnout* for the public hearing on the education reforms?

once in a blue moon: rarely, infrequently

- ○ Snow falls on the city of San Diego, California, *once in a blue moon.*
- ○ *Once in a blue moon* my wife and I eat at a very expensive restaurant.

to give up: to stop trying; to stop a bad habit (S); to surrender (S)

- ○ I'm sure that you can accomplish this task. Don't *give up* yet!
- ○ If you *give up* smoking now, you can certainly live a longer life.

○ The soldiers *gave* themselves *up* in the face of stronger enemy forces.

to cross out: to cancel by marking with a horizontal line (S)

○ The teacher *crossed out* several incorrect words in Tanya's composition.

○ I *crossed* the last line *out* of my letter because it had the wrong tone to it.

to take for granted: not to appreciate fully (S); to assume to be true without giving much thought (S)
A noun or pronoun often follows the verb *take*.

○ John *took* his wife *for granted* until once when he was very sick and needed her constant attention for a week.

○ He spoke English so well that I *took* it *for granted* he was an American.

○ He *took for granted* that I wasn't American because I spoke English so poorly!

to take into account: to consider a fact while evaluating a situation (S)
Again, a noun or pronoun often follows the verb *take*.

○ The judge *took* the prisoner's young age *into account* before sentencing him to three months in jail.

○ Educators should *take into account* the cultural backgrounds of students when planning a school curriculum.

to make clear: to clarify, to explain (S)

○ Please *make clear* that he should never act so impolitely again.

○ The supervisor *made* it *clear* to the workers that they had to increase their productivity.

clear-cut: clearly stated, definite, apparent

○ The president's message was *clear-cut:* the company had to reduce personnel immediately.

○ Professor Larsen is well known for his interesting and *clear-cut* presentations.

to have on: to be wearing (S)

- How do you like the hat which Grace *has on* today?
- When Sally came into the room, I *had* nothing *on* except my shorts.

to come to: to regain consciousness; to equal, to amount to

- At first they thought that the man was dead, but soon he *came to*.
- The bill for groceries at the supermarket *came to* fifty dollars.

to call for: to require; to request, to urge

- This cake recipe *calls for* some baking soda, but we don't have any.
- The members of Congress *called for* new laws to regulate the banking industry.

Choose the appropriate idiomatic expression to substitute for the italicized word or words in each sentence below. Idioms from previous lessons are indicated by number.

1. The majority of the investors at the shareholders' meeting *urged* the resignation of the chairman of the board.

   a. called for
   b. took for granted
   c. called on (Lesson 2)

2. How many people *appeared* for the baseball game yesterday?

   a. turned out
   b. came to
   c. turned around (Lesson 8)

3. My reason for voting "no" is very *apparent:* I disagree completely with the position of other committee members on this matter.

    a. once in a blue moon
    b. clear-cut
    c. made clear

4. There was a big traffic jam on the freeway when a truck *stopped functioning* in one of the middle lanes.

    a. burned down (Lesson 12)
    b. gave up
    c. broke down

5. Mrs. Thomas was very surprised when she received the bill for her hospital stay. It *equalled* almost ten thousand dollars.

    a. crossed out
    b. came from (Lesson 10)
    c. came to

6. Aaron *had the habit to* drink a lot of beer until he decided to lose weight.

    a. is used to (Lesson 9)
    b. gave up
    c. used to (Lesson 9)

7. That's a very nice dress that you *are wearing.* Where did you buy it?

    a. have on
    b. take into account
    c. take for granted

8. As it *resulted,* I didn't have to worry about the game; we won it easily.

    a. turned out
    b. made clear
    c. was over (Lesson 7)

9. The gang of criminals *surrendered* to the police after eight hours of hiding in the warehouse.

    a. crossed out
    b. gave up
    c. looked out (Lesson 5)

10. Joe's mother *considered the fact* that Joe was trying to help his brother when the accident took place.

    a. took for granted
    b. made clear
    c. took into account

Fill in each blank with the appropriate form of an idiomatic expression from this unit only.

Mrs. Lee: Hello. How are you?

Cashier: Fine, ma'am. Only buying a few groceries today, I see.

Mrs. Lee: Yes. As it _____, I only have a few dollars with me.

Cashier: That blouse you _____ really goes nicely with your skirt.

Mrs. Lee: Thank you. I just bought it this morning.

Cashier: Oh, no!

Mrs. Lee: What's the matter?

Cashier: I can't continue using the cash register. It just

_____.

Mrs. Lee: That's terrible. Does this happen very often?

Cashier: Not at all. In fact, it happens only

_____. Unfortunately, this kind of situation usually

_____ for the manager's assistance, but he's not here right now.

Mrs. Lee: Just when you _____ that something like this won't happen, it does!

Cashier: I guess I have to figure out your bill with paper and pencil. Let's see—the total for your purchases _____ $13.35.

Mrs. Lee: Did you _____ my discount coupons?

Cashier: No, I forgot. Thanks for reminding me.

L E S S O N 14

to eat in/to eat out: to eat at home/to eat in a restaurant

- ○ I feel too tired to go out for dinner. Let's *eat in* again tonight.
- ○ When you *eat out*, what restaurant do you generally go to?

cut and dried: predictable, known beforehand; boring

- ○ The results of the national election were rather *cut and dried;* the Republicans won easily.
- ○ A job on a factory assembly line is certainly *cut and dried.*

to look after: to watch, to supervise, to protect (also: **to take care of, to keep an eye on**)

- ○ Grandma will *look after* the baby while we go to the lecture.
- ○ Who is going to *take care of* your house plants while you are away?
- ○ I'd appreciate it if you'd *keep an eye on* my car while I'm in the store.

to feel like: to have the desire to, to want to consider
This idiom is usually followed by a gerund (the *-ing* form of a verb used as a noun).

- ○ I don't *feel like* studying tonight. Let's go to a basketball game.
- ○ I *feel like* taking a long walk. Would you like to go with me?

once and for all: finally, absolutely

- ○ My daughter told her boyfriend *once and for all* that she wouldn't date him anymore.
- ○ *Once and for all*, John has quit smoking cigarettes.

Essential Idioms in English **71**

to hear from: to receive news or information from

To hear from is used for receiving a letter, telephone call, etc., from a person or organization.

- ○ I don't *hear from* my brother very often since he moved to Chicago.
- ○ Have you *heard from* the company about that new job?

to hear of: to know about, to be familiar with; to consider

The second definition is always used in the negative.

- ○ When I asked for directions to Mill Street, the police officer said that she had never *heard of* it.
- ○ Byron strongly disagreed with my request by saying, "I won't *hear of* it!"

to make fun of: to laugh at, to joke about

- ○ They are *making fun of* Carla's new hair style. Don't you think that it's really strange?
- ○ Don't *make fun of* Jose's English. He's doing the best he can.

to come true: to become reality, to prove to be correct

- ○ The weatherman's forecast for today's weather certainly *came true*.
- ○ Everything that the economists predicted about the increased cost of living has *come true*.

as a matter of fact: really, actually (also: **in fact**)

- ○ Hans thinks he knows English well but, *as a matter of fact*, he speaks very poorly.
- ○ I didn't say that. *In fact*, I said quite the opposite.

to have one's way: to arrange matters the way one wants (especially when someone else doesn't want the same way) (also: **to get one's way**)

- ○ My brother always wants to *have his way*, but this time our parents said that we could do what I wanted.
- ○ If Sheila doesn't *get her way*, she becomes very angry.

to look forward to: to expect or anticipate with pleasure
This idiom can be followed by a regular noun or a gerund.

○ We're greatly *looking forward to* our vacation in Mexico.

○ Margaret never *looks forward to* going to work.

Choose the appropriate idiomatic expression to substitute for the italicized word or words in each sentence below.

1. I asked my neighbor *to watch* my dog while I was out of town.

   a. to come to (Lesson 13)
   b. to make fun of
   c. to look after

2. Do you *want to consider* going to a movie tonight?

   a. feel like
   b. stand to reason (Lesson 12)
   c. look forward to

3. I wonder when I'm finally going *to receive news from* Joe.

   a. to hear of
   b. to hear from
   c. to get in touch with (Lesson 9)

4. The teacher told her young student, "Please don't cheat again *from this time into the future.*"

   a. from now on (Lesson 11)
   b. once and for all
   c. as a matter of fact

5. Aren't you glad that we decided *to eat at a restaurant* tonight? This food is great!

   a. to eat in
   b. to take out (Lesson 3)
   c. to eat out

6. The decision to sell the failing business was rather *pre-dictable.*

   a. come true
   b. in fact
   c. cut and dried

7. Barbara is a nice person, but unfortunately she always has *to arrange matters the way she wants.*

   a. to have her way
   b. to make up her mind (Lesson 5)
   c. to come true

8. Are you *pleasantly anticipating* the end of the school semester?

   a. hearing of
   b. looking forward to
   c. paying attention to (Lesson 8)

9. *Actually,* I really don't want to take a break right now. I'd rather continue working.

   a. Little by little (Lesson 2)
   b. As a matter of fact
   c. For good (Lesson 5)

10. Everything that my parents told me about becoming an adult *proved to be correct.*

    a. came true
    b. to hear of it
    c. in fact

Answer these questions orally by making use of the idiomatic expressions studied in this lesson.

1. What famous American actors and actresses have you *heard of?*
2. If you were a parent, what activity would you *not hear of* your small child doing?
3. When was the last time that you *heard from* an old friend from your childhood?
4. Do you prefer to *eat in* or *eat out? How often do you eat out?*
5. Is there anything that you want to stop doing *once and for all?* What?

6. What event in the near future are you *looking forward to?*
7. When might you insist on *having your way* with your friends?
8. How do you feel when other people *make fun of* you?
9. When do you most *feel like* studying—in the morning or in the evening? Why?
10. All people have hopes and desires for the future. What hope or desire do you want most *to come true?*

inside out: with the inside facing the outside

○ Someone should tell little Bobby that his shirt is *inside out.*

○ The high winds ruined the umbrella by blowing it *inside out.*

upside down: with the upper side turned toward the lower side

○ The accident caused one car to turn *upside down,* its wheels spinning in the air.

○ One of the students was only pretending to read her textbook; the teacher could see that the book was actually *upside down.*

to fill in: to write answers in (S); to inform, to tell (S)
For the second definition, the idiom can be followed by the preposition *on* and the information that someone is told.

○ You should be careful to *fill in* the blanks on the registration form correctly.

○ Barry was absent from the meeting, so I'd better *fill* him *in.*

○ Has anyone *filled* the boss *in on* the latest public relations disaster?

to fill out: to complete a form (**S**)

This idiom is very similar to the first definition above. *To fill in* refers to completing various parts of a form, while *to fill out* refers to completing a form as one whole item.

- ○ Every prospective employee must *fill out* an application by giving name, address, previous jobs, etc.
- ○ The teenager had some trouble *filling* the forms *out* by himself, so his mother helped him.

to take advantage of: to use well, to profit from; to use another person's weaknesses to gain what one wants

- ○ I *took advantage of* my neighbor's superior skill at tennis to improve my own ability at the game.
- ○ Teddy is such a small, weak child that his friends *take advantage of* him all the time. They *take advantage of* him by demanding money and making him do things for them.

no matter: regardless of

This idiom is a shortened form of *it doesn't matter*. It is followed by a question word such as *how, where, when, who,* etc.

- ○ *No matter* how much money he spends on his clothes, he never looks well dressed.
- ○ *No matter* where that escaped prisoner tries to hide, the police will find him sooner or later.

to take up: to begin to do or study, to undertake (**S**); to occupy space, time, or energy (**S**)

- ○ After today's exam, the class will be ready to *take up* the last chapter in the book.
- ○ The piano *takes up* too much space in our living room. However, it would *take* too much time *up* to move it right now; so we'd better wait until later.

to take up with: to consult someone about an important matter (**S**)

The important matter follows the verb *take*, while the person consulted follows *with*.

- ○ Can I *take* the problem *up with* you right now? It's quite urgent.

○ I can't help you with this matter. You'll have to *take* it *up with* the manager.

to take after: to resemble a parent or close relative (for physical appearance only, also: **to look like**)

○ Which of your parents do you *take after* the most?
○ Sam *looks like* his father, but he *takes after* his mother in personality.

in the long run: eventually, after a long period of time
This idiom is similar in meaning to *sooner or later* (Lesson 1). The difference is that *in the long run* refers to a more extended period of time.

○ *In the long run*, the synthetic weave in this carpet will wear better than the woolen one. You won't have to replace it so soon.
○ If you work hard at your marriage, you'll find out that, *in the long run*, your spouse can be your best friend in life.

in touch: having contact

○ James will be *in touch* with us soon to relay the details of the plan.
○ I certainly enjoyed seeing you again after all these years. Let's be sure to keep *in touch*.

out of touch: not having contact; not having knowledge of

○ Marge and I had been *out of touch* for years, but then suddenly she called me up the other day.
○ Larry has been so busy that he seems *out of touch* with world events.

EXERCISES

Choose the appropriate idiomatic expression to substitute for the italicized word or words in each sentence below. Idioms from previous lessons are indicated by number.

1. It is a fact of life that older children use *the weaknesses* of their younger brothers and sisters.
   a. take up with
   b. out of touch with
   c. take advantage of

2. If you want the water to come out of the bottle, you have to turn it *so the top is where the bottom was with the upper side facing the lower side.*
   a. inside out
   b. in the long run
   c. upside down

3. Bernice has a determination to do well in every aspect of her work; she never *stops trying* just because the work is difficult.
   a. gives up (Lesson 13)
   b. takes up
   c. takes after

4. *Regardless of* what he says, I don't believe any of the excuses he offers.
   a. As for (Lesson 12)
   b. No matter
   c. As a matter of fact (Lesson 14)

5. Janice just got back from vacation; let's *inform her* on what happened while she was gone.
   a. fill her in
   b. fill her out
   c. think her over (Lesson 4)

6. This assignment is so *boring and predictable* that I'll be finished in a very short time.

   a. out of the question (Lesson 8)
   b. out of touch
   c. cut and dried (Lesson 14)

7. After Larry finished taking art classes, he decided *to begin to study* journalism.

   a. to take up
   b. to take advantage of
   c. to look like

8. Tom and I have been *not having contact* for many years now; I can hardly believe that he just wrote me a letter.

   a. in touch
   b. in the long run
   c. out of touch

9. Whom do you think that Terry *resembles* most—her mother or her father?

   a. look over (Lesson 6)
   b. takes after
   c. fills out

10. Several neighbors called the police as soon as a big fight *became widespread* in the neighborhood.

    a. was carried away (Lesson 11)
    b. took up with
    c. broke out (Lesson 12)

Answer these questions orally by making use of the idiomatic expressions studied in this lesson.

1. Which of your parents do you *take after* in appearance? In personality?
2. What people in your life are you most *in touch* with?
3. Who have you been *out of touch* with for many years?
4. What object *takes up* the most space in your room?
5. What are some good ways that you can *take advantage of* a friend? Some bad ways?

6. What is the difference between *filling* something *in and filling* something *out*?

7. When you apply to college or university, what forms do you have to *fill out*?

8. What kind of life do you want for yourself *in the long run*?

9. If a person has serious mental or emotional problems, whom can this person *take* the problems *up with*?

10. For what reasons might you find yourself wearing a piece of clothing *inside out*?

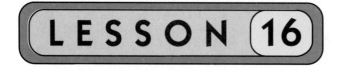

LESSON 16

on one's toes: alert, cautious
This idiom is usually used with the verbs *stay* and *keep*.

○ It's important for all the players on a soccer team to stay *on their toes*.

○ We'd better keep *on our toes* while we're walking along the dark portions of this street.

to get along: to make progress; to manage to live in a certain state of health

○ Juan *is getting along* very well in his English studies.

○ How is Mr. Richards *getting along* after his long illness?

hard of hearing: partially deaf, not able to hear well

○ You'll have to speak a little louder. Mrs. Evans is *hard of hearing*.

○ Please don't shout. I'm not *hard of hearing*.

○ Listening to loud music too much can make you *hard of hearing*.

to see eye to eye: to agree, to concur

○ I'm glad that we *see eye to eye* on the matter of the conference location.

○ A husband and wife don't always *see eye to eye* with each other, but a good marriage can survive small disagreements.

to have in mind: to be considering, to be thinking (S)

○ I don't want to see a movie now. I *have in mind* going to the park.

○ It's up to you what we eat tonight. Do you *have* anything *in mind?*

to keep in mind: to remember, not to forget (S) (also: **to bear in mind**)

○ Please *keep in mind* that you promised to call Stan around noon.

○ I didn't know that Paula doesn't like vegetables. We should *bear* that *in mind* next time we invite her for dinner.

for once: this one time, for only one time

○ *For once* I was able to win a game of golf against Steve, who is a much better player than I am.

○ Dad, *for once* would you please let me drive the new car?

to go off: to explode; to sound as an alarm; to leave suddenly without explanation

○ The accident happened when a box of firecrackers *went off* accidentally.

○ For what time did you set the alarm clock to *go off* tomorrow morning?

○ Vince *went off* without saying good-bye to anybody; I hope he wasn't angry.

to grow out of: to outgrow, to become too old for; to be a result of

○ He still bites his nails now and then, but soon he'll *grow out of* the habit.

○ The need for the salary committee *grew out of* worker dissatisfaction with the pay scale.

to make the best of: to do the best that one can in a poor situation

- ○ If we can't find a larger apartment soon, we'll just have to *make the best of* it right here.
- ○ Even though the Martinez family is having financial problems, they *make the best of* everything by enjoying the simple pleasures of life.

to cut off: to shorten by cutting the ends (**S**); to disconnect or stop suddenly (**S**)

- ○ The rope was two feet longer than we needed, so we *cut off* the extra length.
- ○ The operator *cut* our long-distance phone conversation *off* after two minutes.

to cut out: to remove by cutting (**S**); to stop doing something (**S**) (for the second definition, also: **to knock it off**)
For the second definition, the idiom is usually separated by the pronoun *it*.

- ○ The child likes to *cut out* pictures from the newspaper and to paste them in a notebook.
- ○ He kept bothering her, so finally she told him to *cut it out*. However, he wouldn't *knock it off* until her larger brother appeared.

EXERCISES

Choose the appropriate idiomatic expression to substitute for the italicized word or words in each sentence below. Idioms from previous lessons are indicated by number.

1. My brother and I are having a lot of arguments these days. We can hardly *agree* on anything.

   a. go off
   b. see eye to eye
   c. have in mind

2. How is old Mrs. Dunham *managing to live* after her hip replacement surgery?

    a. getting along
    b. making the best
    c. getting through (Lesson 11)

3. Teddy's foot size is now so big that he's already *become too old for* these baseball shoes.

    a. on his toes for
    b. cut off
    c. grown out of

4. *This one time* I'd like to win a million dollars in the state lottery, but I'm sure I won't.

    a. So far (Lesson 4)
    b. For once
    c. All along (Lesson 2)

5. Wilma awoke suddenly when her alarm clock *sounded* in the morning.

    a. went on (Lesson 6)
    b. went off
    c. went out (Lesson 8)

6. I can't answer your questions about this problem; go see the supervisor and *consult him about it.*

    a. keep him in mind
    b. take it up with him (Lesson 15)
    c. make the best of him

7. At the end of the break, the teacher had *to suddenly stop* the students' conversations and resume class.

    a. to cut out
    b. to go off
    c. to cut off

8. Even though there are a lot of quiet moments in base- ball, the players on the field should always stay *alert.*

    a. out of touch with them (Lesson 15)
    b. bearing them in mind
    c. on their toes

9. Sarah's negative attitude about life *is a result of* an unhappy childhood.
   a. makes the best of
   b. grows out of
   c. gets along

10. I don't know what you think, but I *am considering* a roller skating party for Billy's birthday.
    a. have in mind
    b. never mind (Lesson 2)
    c. keep in mind

Answer these questions orally by making use of the idiomatic expressions studied in this lesson.

1. Why should you stay *on your toes* while driving a car?
2. How are you *getting along* in your English studies?
3. Is anyone in your family *hard of hearing*? What could possibly make a person *hard of hearing* at an early age?
4. What do you do when you don't see eye to eye with a friend? Do you usually stay calm or get angry during an argument?
5. What should parents *keep in mind* as they raise their children? Did your parents do this?
6. Is there anything in life that you would like to do just *for once?*
7. At what time in the morning does your alarm clock usually *go off?*
8. Name one or more habits that you had as a child that later you *grew out of.*
9. As a child, did you like to *cut out* pictures from newspapers and magazines? What did you do with them?
10. Why might someone say *"Cut it out!"* to you?

to blow out: to explode, to go flat (for tires); to extinguish by blowing (S)

○ On our trip to Colorado, one of the car tires *blew out* when it hit a large hole in the road.

○ Little Joey wasn't able *to blow* all the candles *out,* so his big sister helped him.

to become of: to happen to (a missing object or person)
This idiom is always used in a clause beginning with *what.*

○ What has *become of* my pencil? I had it ten minutes ago, but now I can't find it.

○ I wondered what *became of* you. I looked around the shopping center for two hours, but I couldn't find you at all.

to shut up: to close for a period of time (S); to be quiet, to stop talking
The second definition of this idiom is impolite in formal situations.

○ During the hurricane, all the store owners *shut* their shops *up.*

○ Bob's sister told him to *shut up* and not say anything more about it.

○ The student got into big trouble for telling his teacher *to shut up.*

have got: to have, to possess

○ Curtis *has got* a bad cold. He's sneezing and coughing a lot.

○ How much money *have* you *got* with you right now?

have got to: must (also: **have to**)

○ She *has got to* go to Chicago today to sign the contract papers.

○ I *have to* be back home by two o'clock or my wife will feel ill at ease.

to keep up with: to maintain the same speed or rate as

- ○ Frieda works so fast that no one in the office can *keep up with* her.
- ○ You'll have to walk more slowly. I can't *keep up with you.*

on the other hand: however, in contrast

- ○ Democracies provide people many freedoms and privileges. *On the other hand*, democracies suffer many serious problems such as crime and unemployment.
- ○ My sister takes after my father in appearance. *On the other hand*, I take after my mother.

to turn down: to reduce in brightness or volume (**S**); to reject, to refuse (**S**)

- ○ Please *turn down* the radio for me. It's too loud while I'm studying.
- ○ Laverne wanted to join the military but the recruiting officer *turned* her application *down* because Laverne is hard of hearing in one ear.

fifty-fifty: divided into two equal parts

- ○ Let's go *fifty-fifty* on the cost of a new rug for our apartment.
- ○ The political candidate has a *fifty-fifty* chance of winning the election.

to break in: gradually to prepare something for use that is new and stiff (**S**); to interrupt (for the second definition, also: **to cut in**)

- ○ It is best to *break* a new car *in* by driving it slowly for the first few hundred miles.
- ○ While Carrie and I were talking, Bill *broke in* to tell me about a telephone call.
- ○ Peter, it's very impolite to *cut in* like that while others are speaking.

a lost cause: a hopeless case, a person or situation having no hope of positive change

- ○ It seems that Charles will never listen to our advice. I suppose it's *a lost cause.*

○ The police searched for the missing girl for two weeks, but finally gave it up as *a lost cause.*

○ Children who have committed several crimes as teenagers and show no sorrow about their actions are generally *lost causes.*

above all: mainly, especially

○ *Above all*, don't mention the matter to Gerard; he's the last person we should tell.

○ Sheila does well in all her school subjects, but *above all* in mathematics. Her math scores are always over 95 percent.

EXERCISES

Choose the appropriate idiomatic expression to substitute for the italicized word or words in each sentence below. Idioms from previous lessons are indicated by number.

1. The last racehorse wasn't able *to maintain the same speed as* the other horses in the race.

   a. to keep up with
   b. to cut in
   c. to keep track of (Lesson 11)

2. There's only one piece of pie left. Would you like to share it *in two equal parts?*

   a. above all
   b. fifty-fifty
   c. a lost cause

3. We haven't heard from Mike recently. I wonder how he's *progressing* since joining the army.

   a. getting along (Lesson 16)
   b. getting used to (Lesson 9)
   c. breaking in

to be bound to: to be certain to, to be sure to

This idiom is used when the occurrence of an event seems inevitable or unavoidable.

- ○ We *are bound to* be late if you don't hurry up.
- ○ With the economy improving now, their business *is bound to* make more money this year.

for sure: without doubt (also: **for certain**)

- ○ In the dark, I couldn't tell *for sure* whether it was Polly or Sarah who drove by.
- ○ I know *for certain* that Gene will move back to Washington next month.

to take for: to perceive or understand as (S)

This idiom is usually used when someone is mistakenly perceived. A noun or pronoun must separate the idiom.

- ○ Because of his strong, muscular body, I *took* him *for* a professional athlete. As it turns out, he doesn't play any professional sports.
- ○ What do you *take* me *for*—a fool? I don't believe what you're saying at all.

to try out: to test, to use during a trial period (S)

- ○ You can *try out* the new car before you decide to buy it.
- ○ I can let you *try* the computer *out* for a few days before you make a decision.

to tear down: to destroy by making flat, to demolish (S)

- ○ The construction company had to *tear down* the old hotel in order to build a new office building.
- ○ The owners had to *tear* the house *down* after it burned down in a fire.

to tear up: to rip into small pieces (S)

- ○ Deidre *tore up* the letter angrily and threw all the pieces into the trash can.
- ○ He told the lawyer to *tear* the old contract *up* and then to prepare a new one.

to go over: to be appreciated or accepted

This idiom is usually followed by the adverb *well*. (In Lesson 6 this idiom has the meaning *to review*, as in the second sentence of the second example below.)

○ The teacher's organized lessons always *go over* well with her students.

○ The comedian's jokes weren't *going over* well; the audience wasn't laughing much at all. I think that the comedian should go over his material more carefully before each act.

to run out of: to exhaust the supply of, not to have more of

○ We *ran out of* gas right in the middle of the main street in town.

○ It's dangerous to *run out of* water if you are in an isolated area.

at heart: basically, fundamentally
This idiom is used to describe the true character of a person.

○ James sometimes seems quite unfriendly, but *at heart* he's a good person.

○ The Fares often don't see eye to eye, but *at heart* they both love each other very much.

about to: ready to, just going to

○ We were *about to* leave the house when the phone rang.

○ I'm sorry that I broke in. What were you *about to* say?

EXERCISES

Choose the appropriate idiomatic expression to substitute for the italicized word or words in each sentence below. Idioms from previous lessons are indicated by number.

1. We'll have to use the restrooms on the next floor because the ones on this floor are *not in working condition*.

   a. run out of
   b. torn down
   c. out of order (Lesson 6)

2. Jennifer seems unpleasant at times, but *basically* she's a kind person.

   a. at heart
   b. for sure
   c. according to

3. The salesperson agreed to let me *test* the computer for an hour or so in the store.

   a. try out
   b. tear up
   c. do without

4. Because of his uniform, he was *perceived as* a police officer, but actually he was just a security guard.

   a. taken for
   b. bound to
   c. looked out (Lesson 5)

5. *On the authority of* the courts, essential government workers cannot go on strike or refuse to perform their jobs.

   a. About to
   b. According to
   c. As a matter of fact (Lesson 14)

6. Don't you hate to see the city *demolish* those old historic buildings, all in the name of progress?

   a. put out (Lesson 6)
   b. tear down
   c. go without

7. I think that you'd better *check by wearing* those pants before you spend so much money on them.

   a. go over
   b. tear up
   c. try on (Lesson 4)

8. I was *ready to* go to bed when someone knocked on my apartment door.

   a. bound to
   b. about to
   c. feel like (Lesson 14)

9. The President's speech *was accepted* so well that all the members of Congress stood up and applauded.

   a. went over
   b. was bound to
   c. found out (Lesson 2)

10. Wes is planning to go with us to Disneyland *without doubt*.

    a. out of the question (Lesson 8)
    b. at last (Lesson 2)
    c. for sure

   Answer these questions orally by making use of the idiomatic expressions studied in this lesson.

1. If you lost your job and didn't have much money, what would you have to *do without*?
2. Why are students in some schools placed in classes *according to* ability?
3. If parents want to raise their children well, what are they *bound to* do?
4. If you see a man leaving a house through a window at night, what might you *take him for*?
5. Why would you be sure to *try out* a car before you buy it?
6. Why might you feel like *tearing up* a letter or some schoolwork?
7. Have you ever said or done something special that *went over* well? What was it?
8. What should you do if you *run out of* energy while you're studying in the evening?
9. Are you a serious person or a fun-loving person *at heart*?
10. What would you do if you were *about to* watch a favorite TV show at home and the telephone rang?

LESSON 19

to bite off: to accept as a responsibility or task
This idiom is often used when one accepts more responsibility than one can handle alone. It is usually used in the form *to bite off more than one can chew.*

- ○ When I accepted the position of chairman, I didn't realize how much I was *biting off.*
- ○ When James registered for 18 units in his last semester at college, he *bit off more than he could chew.*

to tell apart: to distinguish between (also: **to pick apart, to tell from**) (S)

- ○ The two brothers look so much alike that few people can *tell* them *apart.*
- ○ That copy machine is so good that I can't *pick* the photocopy and the original *apart.*
- ○ Most new cars are very similar in appearance. It's almost impossible to *tell* one *from* another.

all in all: considering everything

- ○ There were a few problems, but *all in all* it was a well-organized seminar.
- ○ Leonard got a low grade in one subject, but *all in all* he's a good student.

to pass out: to distribute (also: **to hand out**) (S); to lose consciousness
The verbal idiom *to hand out* can be made into the noun **handout** to refer to items that are distributed in a class or meeting.

- ○ Please help me *pass out* these test papers; there must be a hundred of them.
- ○ Alright, students, here are the class *handouts* for this week.
- ○ The weather was so hot in the soccer stadium that some of the fans in the stands *passed out.*

to go around: to be sufficient or adequate for everyone present; to circulate, to move from place to place

- We thought that we had bought enough food and drink for the party, but actually there wasn't enough to *go around.*
- There's a bad strain of influenza *going around* right now. Have you gotten your flu shots yet?
- Mike has been *going around* telling people that he was accepted to Harvard University. Do you believe him?

to be in (the/one's) way: to block or obstruct; not to be helpful, to cause inconvenience (for both, also: **to get in the/one's way**)

- Jocelyn couldn't drive through the busy intersection because a big truck *was in the way.*
- Our small child tried to help us paint the house, but actually he just *got in our way.*

to put on: to gain (pounds or weight) (S); to present, to perform (S)

- Bob has *put on* a lot of weight recently. He must have *put* at least fifteen pounds *on.*
- The Youth Actor's Guild *put on* a wonderful version of Romeo and Juliet at the Globe Theater.

to put up: to construct, to erect (S); to lift, to raise upwards (S)

- The construction company is tearing down that old office building in order to *put up* a new one.
- Please *put* your hand *up* if you have never studied English grammar before.

to put up with: to tolerate, to accept unwillingly

- The employee was fired because his boss could not *put up with* his mistakes any longer.
- While I'm studying, I can't *put up with* any noise or other distractions.

in vain: useless, without the desired result

- ○ All the doctors' efforts to save the injured woman were *in vain*. She was declared dead three hours after being admitted to the hospital.
- ○ We tried *in vain* to reach you last night. Is your phone out of order?

day in and day out: continuously, constantly (also: **day after day**; for longer periods of time, **year in and year out** and **year after year**)

- ○ During the month of April, it rained *day in and day out*.
- ○ *Day after day* I waited for a letter from him, but one never came.
- ○ *Year in and year out*, the weather in San Diego is the best in the nation.

to catch up: to work with the purpose of fulfilling a requirement or being equal to others
The idiom is often followed by the preposition *with* and a noun phrase. It is similar in meaning to *to keep up with* from Lesson 17.

- ○ The student was absent from class so long that it took her a long time *to catch up*.
- ○ If you are not equal to others, first you have *to catch up with* them before you can *keep up with* them.

EXERCISES

Choose the appropriate idiomatic expression to substitute for the italicized word or words in each sentence below. Idioms from previous lessons are indicated by number.

1. News *circulated* the office that the company president was being forced to resign.
   - **a.** went over (Lesson 18)
   - **b.** went around
   - **c.** went on (Lesson 6)

2. I'm sorry that I have to *interrupt* while you're talking; there's an important phone call for you, Mr. Mason.

   a. break in (Lesson 17)
   b. be in the way
   c. put up with

3. Several students had not been able to keep up with the rest of the class, so they had a lot of difficulty *working to be equal to* the others.

   a. putting on
   b. catching up
   c. picking apart

4. Marsha's efforts to open the door were *useless*; it was tightly shut.

   a. all in all
   b. in vain
   c. no matter (Lesson 15)

5. Jason didn't know anything about carpentry, so he only *caused inconvenience* when he tried to help Tom build a storage room.

   a. put up
   b. passed out
   c. got in the way

6. Get in touch with me when you *return* from your trip, okay?

   a. get back (Lesson 5)
   b. go around
   c. tell from

7. *Considering everything*, I'm lucky to have a steady job, even if it isn't very exciting.

   a. All in all
   b. At all (Lesson 4)
   c. Day in and day out

8. The Lawsons couldn't *tolerate* the noise of the busy highway next to their house any longer, so they decided to move.

   a. put up
   b. put up with
   c. put out (Lesson 6)

9. Is there beer and wine *to be sufficient for everyone*, or should we drive down to the store for more?

   a. to pass out
   b. to go around
   c. to pick apart

10. The magician *performed* an amazing act for the audience of young people.

   a. bit off
   b. called for (Lesson 13)
   c. put on

Answer these questions orally by making use of the idiomatic expressions studied in this lesson.

1. Have you ever *bitten off more than you could chew*? Explain the situation.
2. In what part of the world is it difficult to *tell* night and day *apart*?
3. Have you ever *passed out* or seen someone *pass out*? What happened?
4. What do people in an audience have to do if there are not enough seats to *go around*?
5. What should you tell someone who is *in your way* while you're working?
6. How could someone *put on* a lot of weight in a short time?
7. In class, when would you *put up* your hand? Is this easy or difficult for you to do? Why?
8. What are some of the things in life that you have trouble *putting up with*?

9. How would you feel if you had to stay at home *day in and day out* taking care of the housework and, perhaps, children? Would you feel satisfied or would you feel unhappy? Explain your reasons.

10. Have you ever found yourself *catching up* with others? What was the situation?

LESSON 20

to hold still: not to move (S)
- ○ Please *hold still* while I adjust your tie.
- ○ If you don't *hold* that camera *still*, you'll get a blurred picture.

to know by sight: to recognize (S)
This idiom is used when the *person* has been seen previously but is not known personally. The *person* must be used to separate the idiom.
- ○ I have never met our new neighbors; I simply *know* them *by sight*.
- ○ The woman said that she would *know* the thief *by sight* if she ever saw him again.

to be the matter: to be unsatisfactory, to be improper, to be wrong
In a question, this idiom is used with *what or something*. In an answer, *something* or *nothing* is usually used.
- ○ A: What *is the matter*, Betty? You look very upset.
- ○ B: Yes, something *is the matter*. I've lost my purse!
- ○ A: *Is something the matter*, Charles? You don't look well.
- ○ B: No, nothing *is the matter*. I'm just a little under the weather.

to bring up: to rear, to raise from childhood (**S**); to mention, to raise an issue, to introduce a topic (**S**)

- ○ Parents should *bring up* their children to be responsible members of society.
- ○ Sarah wanted to *bring* the scheduling problem *up* at the club meeting, but finally she decided against doing so.
- ○ One of the students *brought up* an interesting point related to the subject in our textbook.

to get lost: to become lost; to go away in order not to bother The second definition provides a very informal, even rude, meaning that should be used only with close friends. It is sometimes used in a joking manner.

- ○ While driving in Boston, we *got lost* and drove many miles in the wrong direction.
- ○ Todd kept bothering me while I was studying, so I told him to *get lost*.
- ○ Lisa joked that she wanted her sister to *get lost* forever.

to hold up: to delay, to make late (**S**); to remain high in quality

- ○ A big accident *held up* traffic on the highway for several hours.
- ○ Deidre is amazed at how well her car has *held up* over the years.

to run away: to leave without permission; to escape

- ○ The young couple *ran away* and got married because their parents wouldn't permit it.
- ○ That cat is just like a criminal—it *runs away* from anyone who tries to come near!

to rule out: to refuse to consider, to prohibit (**S**)

- ○ Heather *ruled out* applying to college in Texas because she would rather go to school in Canada.
- ○ I'd like to watch a good movie on TV tonight, but a ton of homework *rules* that *out*.

by far: by a great margin, clearly

- ○ Jacquie is *by far* the most intelligent student in our class.

○ This is *by far* the hottest, most humid summer we've had in years.

to see off: to say good-bye upon departure by train, airplane, bus, etc. (also: **to send off**) (S)
A noun or pronoun must divide the idiom.

○ We are going to the airport to *see* Peter *off* on his trip to Europe.
○ When I left for Cincinnati on a business trip, no one came to the train station to *send* me *off.*

to see out: to accompany a person out of a house, building, etc. (S)
A noun or pronoun must again divide the idiom.

○ The Johnsons were certain to *see* their guests *off* as each one left the party.
○ Would you please *see* me *out* to the car? It's very dark outside.

no wonder: it's no surprise that, not surprisingly
This idiom derives from reducing *it is no wonder that . . .*

○ *No wonder* the portable heater doesn't work. It's not plugged into the electrical outlet!
○ Jack has been out of town for several weeks. *No wonder* we haven't seen him recently.

EXERCISES

Choose the appropriate idiomatic expression to substitute for the italicized word or words in each sentence below. Idioms from previous lessons are indicated by number.

1. This new typewriter isn't *remaining high in quality* as well as the typewriter that I had for over twenty years.
   a. holding still
   b. bringing up
   c. holding up

2. When Tim's roommate asked to borrow Tim's car for the whole weekend, Tim responded jokingly by saying, *"Go away!"*

    a. Get lost
    b. Rule out
    c. Never mind (Lesson 2)

3. The Simpson children were *raised* on a farm, so they have an appreciation of nature that most children don't have.

    a. put up (Lesson 19)
    b. brought up
    c. known by sight

4. Would you like Alex *to accompany you outside* to your car?

    a. to see you off
    b. to see you out
    c. to see you about (Lesson 10)

5. This is the best meal I've ever had in this restaurant *by a great margin.*

    a. by far
    b. little by little (Lesson 2)
    c. by myself (Lesson 3)

6. The company president *refused to consider* the participation of the middle managers in future business negotiations.

    a. brought up
    b. ruled out
    c. was the matter

7. *It's no surprise that* the water is cold. No one turned on the stove!

    a. No matter (Lesson 15)
    b. Nothing is the matter
    c. No wonder

8. I'm sorry I'm late. I was *delayed* by heavy traffic.

    a. taken hold of (Lesson 11)
    b. held up
    c. held still

9. The new flight attendant hesitated *to raise* the issue of overtime pay with the union representative.

   a. to bring up
   b. to be the matter of
   c. to be in charge of (Lesson 9)

10. *Occasionally* Mary enjoys driving up to the mountains and camping by herself.

    a. Over and over again (Lesson 8)
    b. Every now and then (Lesson 10)
    c. Once in a blue moon (Lesson 13)

Answer these questions orally by making use of the idiomatic expressions studied in this lesson.

1. Give an example of when you would have to *hold still*.
2. Why might you choose to introduce yourself to someone that you *know* only *by sight*?
3. Where were you *brought up*? Did your parents *bring you up* well?
4. Are there any topics that you would never *bring up* with your parents? Can you mention any of them?
5. Have you ever *gotten* seriously *lost*? What happened?
6. Could you ever tell someone to *get lost*? Why or why not?
7. Which countries manufacture products that generally *hold up* well?
8. What kind of job would you definitely *rule out* for yourself? Why?
9. When was the last time that someone *saw* you *off*?
10. Why would you offer to *see* someone *out* of your house or apartment?

to go up: to increase (also: **to drive up**); to be constructed, to be erected

The second definition is the same as the one for *to put up* in Lesson 19, except that *to go up* is not used with a noun object.

- ○ Economists are predicting that consumer prices *are going up*. Inflation always has a tendency to *drive up* the cost of products.
- ○ A new office *is going up* in the downtown area. A major construction company is *putting it up*.

to go up to: to approach (also: **to come up to, to walk up to, to run up to, to drive up to,** etc.)

The related forms have the same meaning, but the type of movement is different.

- ○ After the lecture, several people in the audience *went up to* the speaker to congratulate her.
- ○ The little girl *came up to* me and shook my hand as if she had known me for years.
- ○ Bill's friend didn't want to admit that they had gotten lost, but finally he agreed to *drive up to* a gas station and inquire about the correct route.

to hand in: to submit or deliver something that is due (**S**)

- ○ Every student has to *hand in* an original composition each week of the semester.
- ○ All the salespeople *hand* their weekly reports *in* on Friday.

in case: in order to be prepared if

When the idiom occurs at the end of the sentence (the second example), then the meaning is *in order to be prepared if something happens*. The "something" might be an accident, a delay, etc.

- ○ You'd better close the windows *in case* it rains.

○ We should be sure to leave for the airport early, just *in case*.

○ Cynthia, take one of your books *in case* you have some time to read on our trip.

to take apart: to disassemble, to separate the parts of something (S)
A noun or pronoun usually divides this idiom.

○ It is much easier to *take* a watch *apart* than it is to assemble it.

○ The engine had a serious problem, so the mechanic had to *take* it *apart* completely in order to fix it.

to put together: to assemble (S)
A noun or pronoun usually divides this idiom. The preposition *back* is used when something has been disassembled and then is being reassembled, as in the second example.

○ Todd followed the directions on the box but he couldn't manage to *put* the bicycle *together* properly.

○ After the teenager took the broken video game apart and fixed it, he was unable to *put* it *back together* again.

to be better off: to be in a more favorable condition or situation
The opposite of this idiom is **to be worse off.**

○ Jim would *be better off* staying at home because of his cold.

○ You'd *be* much *better off* working in an office than in a factory.

○ The economies of some nations *are worse off* than they were several decades ago.

to be well-off: to have enough money to enjoy a comfortable life, to be rich (also: **to be well-to-do**)

○ They live in the best section of town in a large home; they *are* very *well-off*.

○ By the time I reach the age of fifty-five, I hope to *be well-to-do* and to travel frequently.

to take by surprise: to surprise, to amaze, to astonish (**S**)
A noun or pronoun usually divides this idiom.

- ○ The offer of a high-paying position with another company *took* me *by surprise*.
- ○ The president's announcement that the university was in financial trouble didn't *take* anyone *by surprise*.

to keep in touch with: to maintain contact with (also: **to stay in touch with**)
This idiom should be compared with *to get in touch with* in Lesson 9.

- ○ You can telephone me every few days, and in that way we can *keep in touch with* each other.
- ○ He promised to *stay in touch with* us while he was abroad. However, we were very disappointed that he never did *get in touch with* us.

to name after: to give the same name as another (**S**)

- ○ Helen's parents *named* Helen *after* her grandmother.
- ○ My grandson is *named after* Calvin Coolidge, the 30th President of the United States.

to hold on: to grasp tightly or firmly; to wait, to be patient
The second definition is often used when someone is talking on the telephone.

- ○ The little girl *held on* to her mother's hand and refused to let go as they walked through the large crowd of people.
- ○ (on the telephone) Could you please *hold on* a moment while I get a pencil and paper?
- ○ Come on, Mike, *hold on*. I can't get ready so quickly.

Choose the appropriate idiomatic expression to substitute for the italicized word or words in each sentence below. Idioms from previous lessons are indicated by number.

1. In some countries, *being rich* means just having a home for your family.

   a. being worse off
   b. being well-off
   c. being up to (Lesson 11)

2. Jake was *astonished* when he learned that he had been accepted to Yale University.

   a. taken by surprise
   b. taken apart
   c. better off

3. We'd better take umbrellas with us *to be prepared if* it rains.

   a. on the other hand (Lesson 17)
   b. in case
   c. in time to (Lesson 7)

4. Surono wasn't able *to submit* his assignment to the teacher because he had forgotten to do it.

   a. to put together
   b. to pass out (Lesson 19)
   c. to hand in

5. We've run out of milk so we'll *not be able to have* it at dinnertime.

   a. have on (Lesson 13)
   b. run up to
   c. do without (Lesson 18)

6. Dr. Madison has *assembled* an excellent team of administrators and instructors for the staff of the new community college.

    a. put together
    b. taken apart
    c. gone up

7. Timmy, I asked you *to be patient* a moment while I finish getting dressed.

    a. to take hold of (Lesson 11)
    b. to hold on
    c. to keep in touch with

8. I can't believe how prices are *increasing* more and more every year.

    a. going up to
    b. going up
    c. going off (Lesson 16)

9. Richard went to the library *to locate* information on the Civil War.

    a. to look up (Lesson 4)
    b. to look out (Lesson 5)
    c. to look after (Lesson 14)

10. It makes my parents happy that I *maintain contact with* them while I am away from home attending college.

    a. get along with (Lesson 3)
    b. have to do with (Lesson 8)
    c. keep in touch with

Answer these questions orally by making use of the idiomatic expressions studied in this lesson.

1. Is the cost of living *going up* in your country? What factors can *drive up* prices?

2. Have you ever *gone up to* a famous person and asked for an autograph? (An *autograph* is the signature of a famous person.)

3. Do you always *hand in* assignments in class on time, or are you sometimes late? Do you ever forget to *hand* them *in*?

4. What would you do *in case* the brakes in your car failed while you were driving?

5. As a child, did you enjoy *taking* things *apart?* What kinds of things did you *take apart?*

6. After you took them apart, did you always *put* them *together* again? Were you always successful?

7. Are you *better off* now than you were five years ago? How?

8. Do you consider yourself *well-off?* If not, do you expect to be *well-off* in the future? How do you expect to accomplish it?

9. When you are away from home, are you careful to *keep in touch with* your family or friends?

10. Are you *named after* somebody? Who?

LESSON 22

to stop by: to visit or stop somewhere briefly in order to do something

- ○ James had to *stop by* the registrar's office to submit a transcript request form.
- ○ Let's *stop by* the supermarket and pick up a few grocery items.

to drop (someone) a line: to write a note to someone (S)

- ○ As soon as I get to Florida, I'll *drop* you *a line* and tell you about my new job.
- ○ If you have time, *drop* me *a line* now and then while you're traveling.

to come across: to meet or find unexpectedly (also: **to run across**); to be perceived or judged as (also: **to come off**)

- ○ While Cheryl was cleaning the attic, she *came across* some very old coins. It took her by surprise to *run across* something like that.

○ Jeff's boss *comes across* as a tough, unpleasant person, but actually Jeff says that he is a good employer. Some people *come off* quite differently than they really are.

to stand for: to represent, to signify; to tolerate
The second definition is usually used in a negative sense. The meaning is the same as *to put up with* in Lesson 19.

○ On the American flag, each star *stands for* one of the fifty states, and each stripe *stands for* one of the original thirteen colonies of the 1800s.

○ The citizens wouldn't *stand for* the increase in crime in their city, so they hired more police officers and built another jail.

to stand a chance: to have the possibility of accomplishing something
This idiom is often used with an adjective such as *good* or *excellent*. It also occurs in the negative, sometimes with the adjective *much*.

○ The New York baseball team *stands a good chance* of winning the World Series this year.

○ Because John doesn't have any previous work experience, he doesn't *stand a chance* of getting that job.

○ The woman injured in the serious train accident doesn't *stand much chance* of surviving.

to take pains: to work carefully and conscientiously

○ She *takes pains* to do everything well; she's our best employee.

○ He *took* great *pains* with his last assignment because he needed to get an excellent grade to pass the class.

to look on: to watch as a spectator, to observe

○ Hundreds of people were *looking on* as the police and firefighters rescued the passengers in the wrecked train.

○ I stayed with my son at his first soccer practice and *looked on* as the coach worked with the boys.

to look up to: to admire, to respect greatly

- ○ Children will most certainly *look up to* their parents if the children are brought up well.
- ○ Everyone *looks up to* the director of our department because he is a kind and generous person.

to look down on: to feel superior to, to think of someone as less important

- ○ People who are in positions of power should be careful not to *look down on* those who work for them.
- ○ Why does Alma *look down on* Mario just because his family is so poor?

to take off: to leave the ground (for airplanes); to leave, often in a hurry
The noun form **takeoff** derives from this idiom.

- ○ The plane *took off* over an hour late. The passengers had to buckle their seatbelts during *takeoff*.
- ○ Do you have *to take off* already? You just arrived an hour ago!

to pull off: to succeed in doing something difficult (**S**); to exit to the side of a highway

- ○ The group of investors *pulled off* a big deal by buying half the stock in that company. I wonder how they *pulled* it *off* before the company could prevent it.
- ○ The motorist *pulled off* when the police officer turned on the red lights and the siren.

to keep time: to operate accurately (for watches and clocks)
This idiom is usually used with adjectives such as *good* and *perfect*.

- ○ Although this is a cheap watch, it *keeps good time*.
- ○ The old clock *keeps perfect time;* it's never fast or slow.

EXERCISES

Choose the appropriate idiomatic expression to substitute for the italicized word or words in each sentence below. Idioms from previous lessons are indicated by number.

1. In computer code, a binary number such as 10010001 *represents* a letter, number, or other character on a computer keyboard.

    a. stands for
    b. looks on
    c. figures out (Lesson 7)

2. The handyman *worked carefully to* paint the house neatly so that it looked like a professional job.

    a. stood a chance to
    b. took off to
    c. took pains to

3. This stopwatch *doesn't operate accurately* at all; you ran a hundred meters in much faster than fifteen seconds.

    a. doesn't keep out (Lesson 11)
    b. doesn't pull off
    c. doesn't keep good time

4. Rhonda has *to briefly visit* the pharmacy in order to get her medication for stomach trouble.

    a. to stop by
    b. to pull off
    c. to come across

5. Did Frieda *write you* after she returned to Germany?

    a. look down on you
    b. drop you a line
    c. look up to you

6. How can you *tolerate* such a mess in your son's bedroom? You should make him wash all those dirty clothes and clean up his room!

    a. put away (Lesson 4)

b. look down on

c. stand for

7. The crowd of political supporters was *greatly affected* by the news of the election victory.

   a. taken off

   b. carried away (Lesson 11)

   c. looked on

8. While Jerry was walking down the sidewalk, he *unexpectedly found* a twenty-dollar bill lying by the side of the road.

   a. came across

   b. came to (Lesson 13)

   c. took off

9. Leah managed *to succeed in winning* an important victory in a statewide track and field competition this year when no one expected her to do so.

   a. to come off

   b. to pull off

   c. to take off

10. However, I'm afraid that Leah doesn't *have the possibility* of winning a medal in the Olympic Games next year.

    a. stand a chance

    b. stand for

    c. stand to reason (Lesson 12)

Answer these questions orally by making use of the idiomatic expressions studied in this lesson.

1. If you had to buy a birthday card, what kind of store would you *stop by?*

2. Are you always certain to *drop* your friends *a line* when you travel? Why or why not?

3. What would you do if you *came across* a bag containing a large amount of money?

4. When giving a talk or lecture to an audience, how would a speaker want to *come across?*

5. What do the initials U.S.A. *stand for?* Are there initials that *stand for* your country? What are they?

6. What kind of person *stands a chance* of becoming a country's leader? (consider a president, king, dictator, etc.)

7. Do you prefer to be involved in playing a sport or just *looking on?* Why?

8. Whom do you *look up to* most in life? Why?

9. What kind of a person would you *look down on?* Should you avoid feeling this way, or is it sometimes all right?

10. When might you want to, or have to, *take off* from a party early? Have you ever done this?

LESSON 23

to make do: to manage, to cope
This idiom is used when a person must accept a substitute that is not the most suitable.

- ○ Pearl doesn't have a clean blouse so she has to *make do* with the one she wore yesterday.
- ○ During difficult economic times, many people have to *make do* with less.

to give birth to: to bear a human being or animal

- ○ Jane's mother has just *given birth to* twin girls.
- ○ The zoo's Siberian tiger just *gave birth to* a baby cub.

close call: a situation involving a narrow escape from danger (also: **close shave**)

- ○ Bob, that car nearly hit us! What a *close call*.
- ○ We had a *close call* when a small fire in our kitchen almost spread to the rest of the house.

to get on one's nerves: to annoy or disturb (also: **to bug**)

- ○ Laura loves to talk to anyone. Sometimes her chatter really *gets on my nerves*.
- ○ Jack asked his neighbor to turn down the stereo because it was *bugging* him and he couldn't concentrate.

to put down: to suppress, to quell (S); to criticize unfairly (S)

- ○ The police arrived just in time to *put down* the disturbance before it got very serious.
- ○ Fred tries his best at playing tennis. You shouldn't *put him down* like that.

to go for: to be sold at a certain price; to seek or strive for

- ○ This dress probably *goes for* about $50, don't you think?
- ○ Peter was *going for* first place in the swim meet, but he wasn't able to do better than third place.

to go in for: to have as an interest, such as a sport or hobby (also: **to go for, to be into, to get into**)

- ○ Hal *goes in for* tennis while his wife *goes for* painting and sculpture.
- ○ What sports *are* you *into*? I don't have any time to *get into* sports.

to stay up: to remain awake, not to go to bed

- ○ I want to *stay up* tonight and watch a late movie on TV.
- ○ He *stays up* every night until after one o'clock, preparing his homework.

to stay in: to remain at home, not to go out
An idiom with the opposite meaning is **to stay out.**

- ○ On a rainy day, I like to *stay in* and read.
- ○ Young people are able to *stay out* late at night and get very little sleep.

to take over: to assume control or responsibility for (S); to do or perform again (S)
The meaning of the second definition is almost the same as *do over* in Lesson 11. Also for the second definition, a noun or pronoun must divide the idiom.

- ○ That large investment company specializes in *taking over* smaller businesses that are in financial trouble.
- ○ Most students didn't do well on the important test, so the instructor let them *take* it *over.*

○ Little Mikey didn't have much chance to hit the base-ball during practice, so the coach let him *take* his turn *over*.

to show up: to appear, to arrive; to be found or located (also for the second definition: **to turn up**)

○ It really gets on my nerves that Ursula *shows up* late for every meeting.
○ Willie hopes that the watch he lost last Sunday *shows up* soon.
○ We've looked everywhere for that book, but it hasn't *turned up* yet.

to clean out: to empty, to tidy by removing (S); to steal, to rob (S); to buy or purchase all of something (S)

○ It's time for you to *clean out* your closet so that you can store more things in there.
○ A burglar entered my apartment while I was gone and *cleaned* me *out*. He took over $200 in cash and jewelry.
○ Thousands of shoppers *cleaned out* the store that had gone bankrupt and was selling all its remaining products at very reduced prices.

E X E R C I S E S

Choose the appropriate idiomatic expression to substitute for the italicized word or words in each sentence below. Idioms from previous lessons are indicated by number.

1. The instructor allowed the student *to do* the class *again* because he had received a letter grade of *D* the first time.

   a. to do without (Lesson 18)
   b. to make do
   c. to take over

2. Last night my husband and I *remained awake* until after midnight waiting for my daughter to return from a date.

   a. stayed in
   b. stayed up
   c. showed up

3. David doesn't *have a possibility* of winning enough money in Las Vegas to buy a new car. He's just wasting his time by gambling.

   a. have a close call
   b. stand a chance (Lesson 22)
   c. be better off (Lesson 21)

4. We should get our refrigerator repaired soon. The rattling noise really *disturbs me.*

   a. turns me up
   b. puts me down
   c. gets on my nerves

5. Mr. Fulsom was late leaving his office because a last-minute telephone call *delayed him.*

   a. took him over
   b. held him up (Lesson 20)
   c. went in for him

6. Thousands of customers cleaned out the department store because everything *was being sold for* a very cheap price.

   a. was going for
   b. was going in for
   c. was coming to (Lesson 13)

7. The other students in Judy's class *criticize her unfairly* because she enjoys doing homework and helping the teacher.

   a. put her down
   b. go in for her
   c. take her apart (Lesson 21)

8. Are there enough drinks *to be sufficient for everyone*, or should I go to the kitchen to make more?

   a. to go in for
   b. to make do
   c. to go around (Lesson 19)

9. When Ralph *appears*, we'll discuss the matter of the missing funds.

   a. cleans out
   b. shows up
   c. stays in

10. I can't believe what a *narrow escape* it was when the car went off the road and passed within a few feet of us.

   a. lost cause (Lesson 17)
   b. first-rate (Lesson 10)
   c. close call

Answer these questions orally by making use of the idiomatic expressions studied in this lesson.

1. If your car is broken but you still need to get to work, how would you *make do*?
2. Describe a *close call* that you, or someone you know, has had.
3. When might babies or small children *get on your nerves*?
4. What sports or hobbies do you *go in for*?
5. How late do you usually *stay up*?
6. Why might you decide to *stay in* instead of going out?
7. For what reasons might large businesses *take over* smaller businesses?
8. Why would someone have to *take* a class *over?* Has this ever happened to you?
9. In the United States, when should you generally *show up* for a business meeting? When should you *show up* for a casual party?
10. What would be a good reason for *cleaning out* a garage?

to knock out: to make unconscious **(S)**; to impress or attract greatly **(S)**
This idiom can be made into the noun form **knockout** for both definitions.

○ The prizefighter *knocked out* his opponent with one punch in the first five seconds of the first round. It was the fastest *knockout* in boxing history.

○ Linda's beautiful appearance and slender figure really *knock* me *out*. Isn't she a real *knockout* tonight?

to knock oneself out: to work very hard (sometimes too hard) to do something
A reflexive pronoun must divide the idiom.

○ She really *knocked herself out* trying to pass that difficult class.

○ Don't *knock* yourself *out* during practice. Save your strength for the competition later.

to carry out: to accomplish, to execute **(S)** (also: **to go through with**)

○ It's easy to write down a plan for losing weight, but much harder to *carry* it *out*.

○ Charles promised to *go through with* his plan to enroll in graduate school and get an advanced degree.

to run into: to meet someone unexpectedly; to crash or collide into (also: **to bump into**)

○ It was a shock to *run into* an old friend from high school recently.

○ The drunk driver was slightly injured when he *ran into* a telephone pole.

to set out: to start traveling toward a place (also: **to set off, to head out**); to arrange or display neatly (also: **to lay out**) **(S)**

- ○ We *set out* for the top of the mountain at dawn. Unfortunately, as we *set off*, it started to snow heavily, so we decided to head out again later.
- ○ The children tried to *set out* the dishes on the table, but their dad had to help to *lay* the dishes *out* properly.

to set out to: to intend to, to act purposefully to

- ○ We *set out to* paint the house in one day, but quickly realized that it would be impossible to do so.
- ○ Janet *set out* to compete for the large scholarship grant by writing a good essay.

to draw up: to create by drawing, such as a map **(S)**; to prepare documents or legal papers **(S)**

- ○ Max asked me to *draw up* a map to the party so that he wouldn't get lost.
- ○ Our lawyer agreed to *draw* the contract *up* as soon as possible.

give and take: compromise, cooperation between people

- ○ *Give and take* is an important element of a successful marriage.
- ○ Most business negotiations involve *give and take* between the parties involved.

to drop out of: to stop attending; to withdraw from
This idiom can be made into the noun form **dropout**.

- ○ Some students *drop out of* secondary school early in order to get jobs. However, such *dropouts* often regret their decision later in life.
- ○ Two more baseball teams have *dropped out of* the youth league due to a lack of players.

to believe in: to accept as true, have faith in

- ○ Some people *believe in* being honest in all human affairs, while others accept the need to lie in order to get one's way.

○ Throughout the history of man, some cultures have *believed in* one god while others have *believed in* the existence of many gods.

to cheer up: to make happier, to feel less sad (S)

○ We all tried to *cheer up* the little boy when he started to cry.
○ After the death of Deanne's husband, it was difficult to *cheer* her *up* at all.

to make sense: to be sensible or reasonable

○ It *makes sense* to wait until a sunny day to visit the park together.
○ That Jimmy ran away from home suddenly doesn't *make sense* to any of us.

EXERCISES

Choose the appropriate idiomatic expression to substitute for the italicized word or words in each sentence below. Idioms from previous lessons are indicated by number.

1. Alberto *has faith in* his own ability to succeed in his new business enterprise.

    a. is in charge of (Lesson 9)
    b. carries out
    c. believes in

2. *Cooperation* is important in all relationships between people, especially those who must live and work together closely.

    a. Making sense
    b. Seeing eye to eye (Lesson 16)
    c. Give and take

3. Cynthia *intended to* finish her term paper in one day, but actually it took her three days.

    a. went through with
    b. set out to
    c. knocked herself out to

4. The bicyclist *collided with* a wall and was scraped up badly.

   a. ran into
   b. run out of (Lesson 18)
   c. put up with (Lesson 19)

5. The student apologized to his teacher for *submitting* the essay late.

   a. handing in (Lesson 21)
   b. dropping out of
   c. carrying out

6. In order to avoid the early morning rush hour traffic, we *started traveling* before dawn.

   a. laid out
   b. set out
   c. went out (Lesson 8)

7. My friends tried *to make me feel happier* when I learned that I couldn't graduate because I had to take one class over.

   a. to make me sense
   b. to cheer me up
   c. to change my mind (Lesson 5)

8. It *isn't reasonable* to ruin one's health by drinking alcohol and smoking cigarettes.

   a. doesn't make a difference (Lesson 3)
   b. doesn't make up your mind (Lesson 5)
   c. doesn't make sense

9. Peter *raised* an important issue regarding the next soccer tournament at the club meeting.

   a. put up (Lesson 19)
   b. brought up (Lesson 20)
   c. drew up

10. Stacy *worked very hard* to prepare a nice meal for her family at their reunion.

    a. set out
    b. carried out
    c. knocked herself out

Answer these questions orally by making use of the idiomatic expressions studied in this lesson.

1. Have you ever been *knocked out*? What happened?
2. Have you ever *knocked yourself out* to accomplish something? What was it?
3. When you set goals for yourself, do you usually *carry* them *out*?
4. When was the last time that you *ran into* someone from your past?
5. Why should a store be careful in how it *sets out* its product displays?
6. Have you *drawn up* a will? Why is it important to do so?
7. Why might an athlete *drop out of* a sporting event? Has this ever happened to you?
8. Do you *believe in* capitalism as an economic system? Why or why not?
9. If someone has just lost a job, what could you do or say to *cheer* him or her *up*?
10. For some people, it *makes sense* to spend most of the extra income they make. Would this be true for you? Why or why not?

LESSON 25

to burst out: to depart quickly (also: **to storm out**); to act suddenly
For the second definition, this idiom is usually followed by a gerund form such as *laughing, crying, singing*, etc.

○ Faye and Debbie were so angry at each other that one of them *burst out* the front door of the house and the other *stormed out* the back door.
○ It was so funny to see a little baby in the audience *burst out* crying when the choir group *burst out* singing at the start of the recital.

to get away: to get free, to escape

- ○ We always try to *get away* from the noise and heat of the city for a month or two each summer.
- ○ No one knows how the suspected criminal *got away* from the police.

to get away with: to avoid punishment for

- ○ Jonathan tries to *get away with* coming late to work almost every day; someday he'll suffer the consequences.
- ○ Terence can't continue to put his friends down like that and expect to *get away with* it forever.

to serve (someone) right: to receive one's just punishment (S)
This idiom is usually used at the beginning of a sentence after the subject *it*. Compare the following examples with those in the previous idiom above.

- ○ It *serves* Jonathan *right* to be fired from his job.
- ○ It *serves* Terence *right* that none of his friends are willing to help him move to a new apartment.

to keep up: to prevent from sleeping (S); to continue maintaining (speed, level of work, condition, etc.) (S)

- ○ Could you please turn down the TV volume? You're *keeping up* the children.
- ○ If we can *keep up* this speed, we should arrive there in about two hours.
- ○ James is so proud of his daughter for getting mostly *A's* in school. He's certain that she can *keep up* the good work.
- ○ The Federal Reserve Bank hopes to *keep* the value of the dollar *up* at least through the rest of the year.

to keep up with: to have current knowledge of; to understand as an explanation
This idiom should be compared to the meaning of *to keep up with* in Lesson 17.

- ○ Evan *keeps up with* world affairs by reading a news magazine each week.

○ I understand a lot of the Spanish language, but I can't *keep up with* the fast conversation in this Mexican film.

to stand out: to be easily visible or noticeable (also: **to stick out**)
This idiom is used for someone or something that is different from all others.

○ Her bright red hair makes her *stand out* from others in the group.
○ Brandon Styles is a tall, distinguished gentleman who *sticks out* in any crowd.

to let on: to reveal or tell what you know, to hint

○ We are going to the movies tonight and we don't want Doris to go. If you see her, make sure not to *let on*.
○ They asked me not to *let on* to Ted that we're planning the birthday party; it's supposed to be a big surprise.

to go wrong: to fail, to result badly

○ Something *went wrong* with the engine, so we had to have the car towed to a garage.
○ Shawn should have been here over an hour ago; I'm certain that something *went wrong*.

to meet (someone) halfway: to compromise with someone

○ Steve wanted $4,500 for his car, and Gwen offered $4,000. They *met* each other *halfway* and agreed on $4,250.
○ After a long process of give and take, the owners of the company agreed to *meet* the workers *halfway* by providing some additional health benefits but no wage increase.

to check up on: to examine with the purpose of determining condition (also: **to check on**)
This idiom has the related noun form **checkup**.

○ The government always *checks up on* the background of employees who are hired for sensitive military projects.

○ The doctor wants me to have a thorough medical *checkup* as part of a preventive medicine program.

to stick up: to point or place upwards (S); to rob (S)

○ You should put some water on your hair. It's *sticking up* in the back.

○ A masked thief *stuck up* a grocery store in the neighborhood last night.

E X E R C I S E S

Choose the appropriate idiomatic expression to substitute for the italicized word or words in each sentence below. Idioms from previous lessons are indicated by number.

1. That professor lectures so quickly that I have trouble *understanding his explanations*.

   a. keeping him up
   b. checking up on him
   c. keeping up with him

2. We hope *to escape* this weekend for some camping in the mountains.

   a. to get away with
   b. to break out (Lesson 12)
   c. to get away

3. That man's purple pants and pink shirt really *are noticeable* from a long distance.

   a. stand out
   b. keep up
   c. stop by (Lesson 22)

4. The government was forced *to assume control of* a failing financial institution.

   a. to take over (Lesson 23)
   b. to burst out
   c. to go wrong

5. You should really *compromise with Sally* and agree to share the cost of the car repairs.

   a. serve Sally right
   b. meet Sally halfway
   c. check on Sally

6. How do you manage *to have current knowledge of* political affairs when you're so busy working?

   a. to let on
   b. to keep up with
   c. to be in charge of (Lesson 9)

7. *Considering everything,* we did a very good job of building that storage room by ourselves.

   a. All along (Lesson 2)
   b. Letting on
   c. All in all (Lesson 19)

8. The heat and humidity *prevented me from sleeping* late into the night.

   a. kept me up
   b. stuck me up
   c. cut me off (Lesson 16)

9. No one in the audience reacted to the comedian's first joke except Tamara, who *acted suddenly by* laughing.

   a. got away with
   b. cut down on (Lesson 9)
   c. burst out

10. Please be sure not *to reveal* that we already know about the change in stock ownership rules that are planned by the company board of directors.

    a. to let on
    b. to stick out
    c. to storm out

Answer these questions orally by making use of the idiomatic expressions studied in this lesson.

1. Why might you *burst out* of a place such as a room, office, apartment, house, etc?
2. What do you like to do when you *get away* for a while?
3. As a child, what did you try to *get away with*? Did you usually succeed, or did your parents usually catch you?
4. Some people think that it *serves someone right* to receive the death penalty for the crime of murder. Do you agree or disagree?
5. What might *keep* you *up* in bed? Do you usually go to sleep easily or with difficulty?
6. Do you try to *keep up with* world events? What is your preferred source of information?
7. In the room that you are in right now, what *stands out the most?*
8. What could *go wrong* during a travel tour of a foreign country?
9. Are you ever willing to *meet* someone *halfway* even after you have made up your mind about something? Why or why not?
10. Why is it important for a doctor to *check up on* your health condition? Do you go to the doctor regularly for a *checkup?*

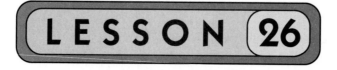

L E S S O N 26

to come about: to happen

○ I didn't find any explanation in the newspaper about how the political coup *came about.*
○ The flood *came about* as a result of the heavy winter rains.

to bring about: to cause to happen

This idiom is used to indicate *who* or *what* caused something to come about.

- ○ John *brought about* the accident because of his carelessness.
- ○ The heavy rains we have each spring *bring about* serious flooding.

to build up: to increase slowly, to make stronger gradually (S)

- ○ They *built up* their savings account so that they could buy a new house.
- ○ The professional athlete exercises regularly to *build* her strength *up*.

to die down: to decrease, to lessen in strength

- ○ The hurricane became a less serious tropical storm when its winds *died down.*
- ○ We let the fire in the fireplace *die down* and enjoyed watching the embers as they glowed in the dark.

to fade away: to diminish gradually in time or distance

- ○ The memory of that unpleasant experience has slowly *faded away.*
- ○ The music of the band gradually *faded away* as the parade passed down the street.

to die out: not to exist anymore; to be in the process of disappearing

- ○ Scientists still are not sure exactly why the dinosaurs *died out.*
- ○ That strange, new style of dancing is slowly *dying out.*

to make out: to read or see clearly (S); to prepare a legal document, such as a will, a check, etc. (S)

- ○ The letter was so poorly handwritten that I couldn't *make out* many of the words.
- ○ Harold, please *make* the check *out* to Acme Piano Company.

to live up to: to fulfill (a standard or promise)

- ○ It was clear that the lazy student would never *live up to* his family's expectations.
- ○ It surprised us that the car salesperson *lived up to* all the promises he made.

to stick to: to adhere to (a promise), to follow or obey (a set of rules, procedures, etc.)

- ○ He made a promise to his wife to quit smoking and drinking, and so far he has *stuck to* it.
- ○ All organizations expect their employees to *stick to* established work rules and procedures.
- ○ If you try hard to *stick to* your principles, then you'll be able to live up to them.

to stick it to: to cheat, to take unfair advantage of (also: **to rip off, the ripoff**)

- ○ Be careful in doing business with that salesperson. He'll *stick it to* you at the first opportunity.
- ○ The car dealership certainly *ripped* me *off* when I bought this car. It has caused me trouble constantly.
- ○ You paid over $400 for that jacket? What a *ripoff!*

to stand up for: to insist on, to demand; to defend, to support

- ○ If you don't *stand up for* your rights in court, the lawyers will try to stick it to you.
- ○ Frank *stood up for* his friend, who was being put down by other teenagers nearby.

to cut corners: to economize, to save money

- ○ Most students live on limited budgets and have to *cut corners* whenever possible.
- ○ The Livingstons have nine children, so it is essential that they *cut corners* at all times.

EXERCISES

Choose the appropriate idiomatic expression to substitute for the italicized word or words in each sentence below. Idioms from previous lessons are indicated by number.

1. The other workers *defended* their co-worker who was accused of stealing from the factory warehouse.

    a. stuck to
    b. stood up for
    c. built up

2. It *is sensible* to check at several dealerships for the best price for a new car model.

    a. makes it clear (Lesson 13)
    b. makes out
    c. makes sense (Lesson 24)

3. The army *fulfilled* the expectations of its commanders by defeating the enemy forces.

    a. lived up to
    b. stuck it to
    c. counted on (Lesson 6)

4. Memories of my youth gradually *diminish* as I grow older.

    a. fade away
    b. build up
    c. come about

5. Some species of animals will *not exist anymore* unless human beings act to save them.

    a. die down
    b. die out
    c. tire out (Lesson 2)

6. After a long illness, Mr. Felson needed time *to slowly increase* his strength again.

    a. to get better (Lesson 7)
    b. to bring about
    c. to build up

Essential Idioms in English   **131**

4. Would Mary be willing *to undertake* a new project even though she's overloaded with work?

   a. to take down
   b. to take on
   c. to take up with (Lesson 15)

5. Please don't *reveal* that you have knowledge of that secret contractual agreement.

   a. take down
   b. give in
   c. let on (Lesson 25)

6. The campers lost on the high mountain were able *to survive* against the cold weather by building a fire and keeping together.

   a. to hold still (Lesson 20)
   b. to hold out
   c. to put out (Lesson 6)

7. I can't attend class tonight, so would you mind *writing notes on* what the instructor says?

   a. running out
   b. taking down
   c. pointing out (Lesson 7)

8. The committee *delayed* in deciding when to have the next board election.

   a. held off
   b. fell behind
   c. called off (Lesson 5)

9. My boss hasn't spoken to me in a week. I wonder if he *feels hostile towards* me because of our conflicting views on the labor negotiations.

   a. has it in for
   b. has it out with
   c. holds out

10. The rescue team was successful in reaching the group of miners trapped deep in the earth before their small supply of air *became exhausted.*

    a. fell behind
    b. burned out (Lesson 12)
    c. gave out

Answer these questions orally by making use of the idiomatic expressions studied in this lesson.

1. What responsibilities do parents *take on* when they decide to have children?
2. Why is it advisable to *take down* what is said during important discussions or talks?
3. When was the last time that an event or plan *fell through* for you?
4. Do you usually *fall behind* in your work, or do you usually keep up with it? Why?
5. When you *have it out with* a friend, do you usually stick to your opinion or do you often *give in*? Why?
6. What are the possible dangers of the pollution that factories *give off*?
7. When you exercise heavily, does your energy quickly *give out*? Why or why not?
8. Have you ever *had it in for* someone? How did you feel, or what did you do?
9. When you *have it out with* someone, do you usually show your emotions clearly, or do you stay calm and control them?
10. How long can a human being *hold out* without food? Without water?

A. Match the idiom in the left column with the definition in the right column.

___	1. once and for all	a. in order to be prepared if
___	2. lost cause	b. especially, mainly
___	3. all in all	c. hopeless situation
___	4. by far	d. eventually
___	5. give and take	e. clearly, by a great margin
___	6. in touch	f. for only one time
___	7. above all	g. compromise, cooperation
___	8. in the long run	h. basically, fundamentally
___	9. close call	i. finally, absolutely
___	10. in case	j. narrow escape from danger
___	11. for once	k. considering everything
___	12. at heart	l. having contact

B. In the space provided, mark whether each sentence is true (**T**) or false (**F**).

1. If a friend doesn't want you *to make fun of* him or her, the friend might tell you *to shut up.* _____

2. If you *run into* someone at the store, you are *sticking to* an appointment. _____

3. If you agree to meet someone *halfway*, it becomes a matter of *give and take.*_____

4. If you want *to keep in touch* with someone, you might decide *to stop by* their place for a while. _____

5. If you have never *heard of* a certain type of animal, you probably *know* it *by sight.* _____

6. If you *fall behind* in your studies because you don't try to *keep up with* the other students, *it serves you right*. _____

7. If something *is going wrong* with your car, then it is *holding up* well. _____

8. If someone *is very well-off*, the person probably has to *cut corners*. _____

9. If you haven't *heard from someone* in a long time, you might *drop* the person a *line*. _____

10. If you really *go in for* a certain sport, you might *set out* to be the best you can at it. _____

11. If you finally *have it out with* someone, you have been *getting along* well with the person. _____

12. If a repairman is trying to fix a complicated watch, he or she would *take pains* to *hold still* while *taking* it *apart*. _____

C. Fill in each blank with the appropriate form of the idioms using *call* listed below. Some expressions come from Lessons 1 to 14.

to call up	to call on	to call off
to call it a day	to call for	close call

1. It was a _____ when the tire blew out on the busy highway.

2. We _____ early because we had been working since six o'clock in the morning.

3. This recipe _____ cream, but there isn't any in the refrigerator. I'll have to stop by the store and pick up some.

4. Margaret _____ her boyfriend almost every day and talks for hours. The telephone bill is her most costly expense.

D. Fill in each blank with the appropriate form of the idioms using *make* listed below. Some expressions come from Lessons 1 to 14.

to make the best of	to make fun of	to make do
to make sense	to make out	to make good time
to make a difference	to make good	to make clear

1. It doesn't _____ to me where we eat out tonight. It's your decision.

2. Children love _____ each other by joking and teasing.

3. It took the Petersons only two hours to go from downtown Los Angeles to San Diego by car. They really _____ on that trip.

4. Could you help me understand this lesson? It doesn't _____ to me.

5. The recipe calls for butter, but I don't have any. I'll just have _____ with margarine.

6. I'm sure that Ted will _____ on his promise to help us with the arrangements for the meeting.

7. Cheryl couldn't _____ the letters on the sign in the distance because it was getting too dark.

8. Did you _____ it _____ to Deborah that she's not welcome at the dinner party? She'd better not show up.

9. There's nothing we can do at this point to change the unfortunate situation. We'll just have _____ it and go on from here.

E. Fill in each blank with the appropriate form of the idioms using *put* listed below. Some expressions come from Lessons 1 to14.

to put on	to put away	to put off
to put out	to put down	to put up with
to put together		

1. Johnny, before you can go outside to play, you have

   _____ all the toys and clothes on the floor of

   your room.

2. There's too much noise in here for me to study. I can't

   _____ it any longer.

3. It's quite cold tonight. I think we should

   _____ some warmer clothing before we go

   outside.

4. Please _____ your cigarette in the ashtray

   immediately. No smoking is allowed in here.

5. I can't _____ doing that important assign-

   ment any longer. It's due in just three days.

6. The military troops used force _____ the

   mass demonstration against the corrupt government.

7. Shari's father helped _____ her new bicycle,

   which came in pieces in a box.

Section 3
Advanced

LESSON 28

to let up: to slacken, to lessen in intensity; to relax or ease one's effort (also: related idiom: **to take it easy**)

○ If the rain doesn't *let up* soon, we won't be able to have our picnic.

○ When Jane is working, she never *lets up* for a moment.

○ Jane should *take it easy* or she'll get exhausted.

to lay off: to abstain from, stop using as a habit; to release or discharge from a job (also: related idiom: **to let go**) (**S**)

○ If you're trying to lose weight, you should *lay off* sweet things.

○ If business continues to be slow, we will have to *lay off* some workers.

○ It will be necessary to *let* the youngest employees *go* first.

to bring out: to show or introduce (to the public) (**S**); to make available (**S**)

○ Most automobile companies *bring out* new models each year.

○ My mother *brought* some snacks *out* for my friends and me to have.

to bring back: to return a bought or borrowed item (also: **to take back**) (**S**)
To bring back is used when you are speaking at the place that an item is bought or borrowed; *to take back* is used when speaking at another place.

○ Ma'am, our store policy is that you can *bring back* the dress as long as you have your sales receipt.

○ You can borrow my car if you promise to *bring* it *back* by six o'clock.

○ I have to *take* this book *back* to the library today.

to wait up for: to wait until late at night without going to bed

- ○ Don't *wait up for* me. I may be back after midnight.
- ○ We *waited up for* our son until two o'clock in the morning before we called the police.

to leave (someone or something) alone: not to disturb, to stay away from (S)(also: **to let alone**)

- ○ *Leave* the baby *alone* for a while and she may go to sleep.
- ○ After the cat had scratched Peter twice, he *let* it *alone*.

let alone: and certainly not (also: **not to mention, to say nothing of**)
Let alone is used after negative forms. The example that follows *let alone* is much less possible than the example that precedes *let alone*.

- ○ I'm too sick today to walk to the kitchen, *let alone* to go to the zoo with you.
- ○ He doesn't even speak his own language well, *let alone* French.

to break off: to terminate, to discontinue (S)

- ○ After war began, the two countries *broke off* diplomatic relations.
- ○ Elsa and Bob were once engaged, but they have already *broken* it *off*.

to wear off: to disappear gradually

- ○ My headache isn't serious. It will *wear off* after an hour or so.
- ○ The effect of the painkilling drug didn't *wear off* for several hours.

to wear down: to become worn gradually through use (also: **to wear away, to wear through**) (S)
Compare with **to wear out** (to become useless from wear) in Lesson 8.

- ○ If you drag your feet while you walk, you'll *wear down* your shoes quickly.

○ The pounding of ocean waves against the coast gradually *wears* it *away*.

○ Johnny has *worn through* the seat of his pants.

○ Helga threw away that dress because she had *worn* it *out*.

on the whole: in general, in most ways (also: **by and large**)

○ He is, *on the whole*, a good student.

○ *By and large*, I agree with your suggestions.

touch and go: risky, uncertain until the end

○ The complicated medical operation was *touch and* go for several hours.

○ The outcome of the soccer final was *touch and go* for the entire match.

Substitute an idiomatic expression for the word or words in italics, making any necessary grammatical changes as well. Then complete each sentence appropriately with your own idea. Also try to use idioms from previous lessons.

Example:

1. Mary *discontinued* her relationship with Paul because she couldn't . . .

   Mary broke off her relationship with Paul because she couldn't put up with him anymore.

2. The effect of the wine *disappeared gradually* after I . . .

3. I think that we should *wait without going to bed* for our daughter until she . . .

to have one's heart set on: to desire greatly, to be determined to

- She *has her heart set on* taking a trip abroad. She's been thinking about it for months.
- Todd *has his heart set on* going to medical school and becoming a doctor.

to buy up: to buy the complete stock of (S)

- Before the hurricane struck, residents *bought up* all the food and water in local stores.
- The government plans to *buy up* all surplus grain in order to stabilize the price.

to buy out: to purchase a business or company (S); to purchase all of a person's shares or stock (S)
This idiom is similar in meaning to *to take over* in Lesson 23.

- Larger companies often *buy out* smaller companies that are having financial difficulties.
- Mr. Lee has been trying for some time to *buy* his partner *out* so that he can control the company by himself.

to sell out: to sell all items (S); to arrange for the sale of a company or business (S)

- That store is closing its doors for good and is *selling out* everything this weekend.
- If my new business enterprise is successful, I'll *sell* it *out* for a few million dollars.

to catch on: to become popular or widespread; to understand, to appreciate a joke
This idiom is often used with the preposition *to* for the second definition.

- Fashions of the past often *catch on* again among young people.
- When the teacher speaks quickly like that, can you *catch on* easily?
- His joke was very funny at the time, but when I told it to others later, nobody seemed to *catch on*. I had to tell the joke again before anyone could *catch on to* it.

to be cut out for: to have the necessary skills or talent for
This idiom is most often used in the negative or in questions.

- ○ John *is* certainly not *cut out for* the work of a trial lawyer.
- ○ Are you certain that you *are cut out for* that kind of job?

to throw out: to discard (S); to remove by force (S); to refuse to consider, to reject (S)

- ○ Instead of *throwing out* our paper waste in the office, we should recycle it.
- ○ When a fight broke out between two people on the dance floor, the management *threw* them *out*.
- ○ The judge *threw* the case *out* because there was insufficient evidence to try the defendant successfully.

to throw up: to erect or construct quickly (S); to vomit (S)

- ○ The Red Cross *threw up* temporary shelters for the homeless victims of the earthquake.
- ○ The ill patient is unable to digest her food properly, so she is *throwing* all of it *up*.

to clear up: to make understandable (also: **to straighten out**)(S); to become sunny

- ○ The teacher tried to *clear up* our confusion about the meaning of the difficult paragraph in the reading.
- ○ It's rather cloudy this morning. Do you think that it will *clear up* later?

E X E R C I S E S

Substitute an idiomatic expression for the word or words in italics, making any necessary grammatical changes as well. Then complete each sentence appropriately with your own idea. Also try to use idioms from previous lessons.

1. After Jane *exercised* for an hour at the gym, she . . .

to dry up: to lose, or cause to lose, all moisture (S); to be depleted

- ○ Every summer the extreme heat in this valley *dries* the stream *up*.
- ○ All funds for the project *dried up* when the local government faced a budget crisis.

to dry out: to lose, or cause to lose, moisture gradually (S); to stop drinking alcohol in excess (also: **to sober up**)

- ○ Martha hung the towel outside on the clothesline in order to *dry it out*.
- ○ Some people go to alcohol recovery centers in order to *dry out*.

to be up to (something): to be doing something; to be planning or plotting something, scheming
The first definition usually takes the form of a question.

- ○ Hi, Jake. I haven't seen you in a long time. What have you *been up to?*
- ○ Those boys hiding behind the building must *be up to* something bad.

to beat around the bush: to avoid discussing directly, to evade the issue

- ○ Our boss *beats around the bush* so much that no one in the office knows exactly what he wants us to do.
- ○ Instead of *beating around the bush*, Melinda explained her objection in very clear terms.

to come to an end: to end, to stop
This idiom is used with *finally* and *never* when some activity lasts too long.

- ○ The meeting finally *came to an end* at ten o'clock in the evening.
- ○ Even though my friend seemed to enjoy the movie, I thought that it would never *come to an end*.

to put an end to: to cause to end, to terminate in a definite manner (also: **to do away with**)

- ○ The dictatorial government *put an end to* organized opposition in the country by making it illegal to form a political party.

○ It may never be possible to *do away with* all forms of prejudice and discrimination in the world.

to get even with: to seek revenge, to retaliate
This idiom is similar in meaning to *to have it in for* in Lesson 27.

○ Bill has had it in for his boss for a long time. He told me he's planning to *get even with* his boss by giving some company secrets to a competitor.

○ I want to *get even with* Steve for beating me so badly in tennis last time. The scores were 6–1 and 6–2.

to fool around: to waste time (also: **to screw around**); to joke, not to be serious

○ The teacher got angry because her students were *fooling around* and couldn't finish their work before the end of class.

○ Sometimes I wish that Pat would stop *fooling around* so much and talk about something more interesting to others.

to look out on: to face, to overlook

○ We really enjoy our new apartment that *looks out on* a river.

○ Their rear window *looks out on* a lovely garden.

to stir up: to cause anger (S); to create (trouble or difficulty) (S)

○ The senseless murder of a small child *stirred up* the whole neighborhood.

○ The boss is in a bad mood today so don't *stir* her *up* with any more customer complaints.

to take in: to visit in order to enjoy (S); to decrease the size of clothes (S); to deceive, to fool (S)

○ We decided to *take in* Toronto on our trip to Canada, and that is where we *took in* the most memorable outdoor stage play we have ever seen.

○ Lois lost so much weight that she had her skirts and slacks *taken in* by her tailor.

○ The fraudulent investment advisor *took* everyone *in* with his sincere manner and generous promises. Most investors lost all their money.

Substitute an idiomatic expression for the word or words in italics, making any necessary grammatical changes as well. Then complete each sentence appropriately with your own idea. Also try to use idioms from previous lessons.

1. Many of the lakes in this part of the country have *lost all moisture* because . . .

2. When I asked Ted what he *was doing,* he responded that . . .

3. Karen hopes this meeting *stops* soon because . . .

4. If the government wants to *terminate* drug abuse in this country, it will have to . . .

5. Ruth *sought revenge on* the girl who stole her boyfriend away from her by . . .

6. Because our son Allen is always *joking,* nobody . . .

7. The house for sale was a valuable piece of property because it *faced* . . .

8. Old-time residents in the neighborhood became *angered* when their new neighbor . . .

9. Marge has lost so much weight in the last month that she has had to *decrease the size of* . . .

10. We visited the San Diego Zoo in order to *visit and enjoy* . . .

Answer these questions orally by making use of the idiomatic expressions studied in this lesson.

1. When driving during rainy weather, why should you *slow down*?

2. Imagine that a country is facing a budget crisis. Which type of government funds are most likely to *dry up* first—those for social programs or those for military programs? Why? What is your opinion about the criteria used in such cases?

3. How might a person with a drinking problem be able to *dry out*? What kinds of problems might keep them from *sobering up*?

4. If someone asked you what you *were up to* these days, how would you respond?

5. How can you tell when young children *are up to* something? Can you remember any personal experience when you were a child?

6. When might someone choose to *beat around the bush*? What could you do to avoid this?

7. What problems in the world would you like to *put an end to*? Do you think that there is hope for this?

8. Has someone ever *stirred* you *up* so much that you wanted to *get even with* him or her? What did you do?

9. What attractions in the area that you are living now have you already *taken in*?

10. Have you ever been *taken in* by someone such as a salesperson or a stranger on the street? What happened?

to go through: to undergo, to experience; to consume, to use (also: **to use up**)

The first definition is used when someone is having some hardship or difficulty.

- ○ I can't believe what she *went through* to get that job. She had four interviews with the hiring committee in one week!
- ○ Frank said that they had *gone through* all the toilet paper in the house, but Steve couldn't believe that they had *used* it all *up*.

to go without saying: to be known without the need to mention

This idiom occurs with a *that*-clause, often with the pronoun *it* as the subject.

- ○ It *goes without saying* that you shouldn't drive quickly in bad weather.
- ○ That he will gain weight if he continues to eat and drink so much *goes without saying*.

to put (someone) on: to mislead by joking or tricking (S)

This idiom is usually used in a continuous tense form. A noun object must divide the idiom.

- ○ Don't worry. I wouldn't expect you do all that work by yourself. I'm just *putting* you *on*.
- ○ Jack can't be serious about what he said. He must be *putting* us *on*.

to keep one's head: to remain calm during an emergency

- ○ When the heater caused a fire, Gloria *kept her head* and phoned for assistance right away; otherwise, the whole house might have burned down.
- ○ When the boat starting sinking in heavy seas, the crew members *kept their heads* and led the passengers to the lifeboats.

to lose one's head: not to think clearly, to lose one's self-control

- When Mel saw a dog in the street right in front of his car, he *lost his head* and drove onto the sidewalk and into a tree.
- If the politician hadn't gotten stirred up and *lost his head*, he never would have criticized his opponent unfairly.

narrow-minded: not willing to accept the ideas of others (the opposite of narrow minded is **broad-minded**)

- *Narrow-minded* people tend to discriminate against groups of people with which they have nothing in common.
- Ted is so *broad-minded* that he has almost no standards by which he judges others.

to stand up: to withstand use or wear; to fail to appear for a date or social engagement (S)

- My old car has *stood up* well over the years. I haven't had any major problems at all.
- Janet was very angry because her new boyfriend *stood* her *up* on their second date. She waited over an hour for him before returning home.

to get the better of: to win or defeat by gaining an advantage over someone

- Jim doesn't seem very athletic at tennis, but if you're not careful, he'll *get the better of* you.
- Lynn gets frustrated when Bruce *gets the better of* her in arguments. No matter what she says, he always has a clever response.

to break loose: to become free or loose, to escape

- During the bad storm, the boat *broke loose* from the landing and drifted out to sea.
- One bicyclist *broke loose* from the pack of racers and pulled ahead towards the finish line.

on edge: nervous, anxious; upset, irritable

○ Cynthia was *on edge* all day about the important presentation she had to give to the local citizens group.

○ I don't like being around Jake when he's *on edge* like that. Someone should tell him to calm down and relax.

to waste one's breath: not be able to convince someone
This idiom is used when someone is wasting time trying to convince another person. The idiom **to save one's breath** is related and means *not to waste effort trying to convince someone.*

○ Don't argue with Frank any longer. You *are wasting your breath* trying to get him to agree with you.

○ I have already decided what I'm going to do. You can't change my mind, so *save your breath.*

to cut short: to make shorter, to interrupt (**S**)

○ The moderator asked the speaker to *cut short* his talk because there wasn't much time remaining for questions from the audience.

○ We were very unfortunate when we received bad news from home that forced us to *cut* our trip *short.*

E X E R C I S E S

Substitute an idiomatic expression for the word or words in italics, making any necessary grammatical changes as well. Then complete each sentence appropriately with your own idea. Also try to use idioms from previous lessons.

1. Mr. Larsen is in the hospital *undergoing* emergency surgery because he . . .

2. When you feel sick, it *doesn't need to be mentioned* that . . .

3. Steve was *misleading me* when he told me that . . .

4. After the serious earthquake, most people *remained calm*, but unfortunately some people . . .

5. You *are not able to convince someone* if he or she is *not willing to accept the ideas of others*, so it is better to . . .

6. Betty *failed to appear for* her date because she . . .

7. Your car will *withstand use* longer if you . . .

8. Our team was able to *win by gaining an advantage over* the other team because . . .

9. The politician was *nervous* before she . . .

10. The meeting was suddenly *interrupted* because . . .

Answer these questions orally by making use of the idiomatic expressions studied in this lesson.

1. Do you *go through* money quickly? What is your biggest expense?
2. Have you ever *gone through* a medical operation? What was it?
3. Do you enjoy *putting* others *on*, or are you a rather serious person?
4. During an emergency, how can you *keep your head*?

5. In what kind of emergency might you be likely to *lose your head?*

6. Do you generally consider yourself to be a *broad-minded* person? In what ways might you be considered a *narrow-minded* person?

7. Which countries are known for manufacturing products that *stand up* well?

8. Have you ever *stood* anyone *up?* What were the circumstances of the situation that caused you to do so?

9. In what sport would an athlete try to *break loose* from an opponent?

10. Does talking in front of a large audience put you *on edge?* Why or why not?

LESSON 32

to step in: to become involved or concerned with something; to enter a place for a brief time (also: **to step into**)

○ When the children started fighting on the playground, a teacher had to *step in* and stop the fight.

○ The supervisor asked one of the employees to *step in* her office for a moment.

○ Would you *step into* the hallway so that I can show you the information posted on the bulletin board?

to step down: to retire or leave a top position, to resign

○ Next May the principal will *step down* after thirty-five years of service to the school.

○ The angry shareholders wanted the company president to *step down* because of the stock scandal.

to step on: to treat severely, to discipline; to go faster, to work more quickly
For the second definition, the idiom is followed by the pronoun *it.*

○ Sometimes it's necessary to *step on* children when they do something dangerous.

○ We're going to be late for the movies. You'd better *step on it!*

a steal: very inexpensive, a bargain
This idiom is often used in an exclamation using *what*.

○ I can't believe that I paid only $2,000 for this three-year-old car. What *a steal!*
○ Scott considered it *a steal* when he bought a complete bedroom set for only $99.

to play up to: to behave so as to gain favor with someone

○ The other students in the class resent Jim because he *plays up to* the teacher in order to get better grades.
○ When my children asked me to go shopping for a new video game, I knew why they had been *playing up to* me all morning.

more or less: approximately, almost; somewhat, to a certain degree

○ Although your bedroom feels smaller, it's *more or less* the same size as mine.
○ Ted *more or less* agreed with our decision to put off the meeting until more members could show up. At least he didn't object strongly.

to screw up: to confuse, to scramble (S); to cause problems in (S)

○ Chris had trouble finding Jane's apartment because the addresses of the buildings *screwed* him *up.*
○ Instead of fixing the television set, the technician *screwed* it *up* even more.

to goof up: to perform badly, to make a mistake (also: **to mess up, to slip up**)

○ I really *goofed up* on the exam today; did you *mess up*, too?
○ Karen *slipped up* when she forgot to deposit money into her checking account.

to go off the deep end: to get very angry and do something hastily

- ○ Just because you had a serious argument with your supervisor, you didn't have to *go off the deep end* and resign, did you?
- ○ When Dan's wife demanded a divorce, he *went off the deep end* again. This time he was shouting so that the whole neighborhood could hear.

to lose one's touch: to fail at what one used to do well

- ○ Milton used to be the best salesman at the car dealership, but recently he seems to have *lost his touch*.
- ○ I used to play tennis very well, but today you beat me easily. I must be *losing my touch*.

in hand: under firm control, well managed

- ○ The copilot asked the pilot if he had the plane *in hand* or whether he needed any help navigating through the severe thunderstorm.
- ○ The police officer radioed to the station that she had the emergency situation *in hand* and didn't require any assistance.

on hand: available, nearby
This idiom is often followed by *in case*.

- ○ I always keep some extra money *on hand* in case I forget to get cash from the bank.
- ○ The concert organizers arranged to have some security guards *on hand* in case there were any problems during the performance.

EXERCISES

Substitute an idiomatic expression for the word or words in italics, making any necessary grammatical changes as well. Then complete each sentence appropriately with your own idea. Also try to use idioms from previous lessons.

1. During the lengthy workers' strike, the police had to *become involved* when . . .

2. After leaving his office down the hall, my supervisor *briefly entered* my office to . . .

3. The old man who founded the company decided to *retire* when . . .

4. Because the mean boss *severely treated* his employees on many occasions, none of them . . .

5. Mike thought that the camera advertised in the newspaper was a *bargain*, so he . . .

6. The children *behaved so as to gain favor with* their parents in order to . . .

7. The young child *caused problems in* his bicycle by . . .

8. Lenny *performed badly* on the physics test because he . . .

9. I hope that the football coach doesn't *get angry and do something hastily* because he seems to be *failing at what he usually does well*; recently his football team . . .

10. The stores in town didn't have enough drinking water *available* after the typhoon, so hundreds of people . . .

Answer these questions orally by making use of the idiomatic expressions studied in this lesson.

1. If someone was being attacked by a thief, would you *step in* and help the person? Why or why not?
2. For what reasons might a top executive of a company *step down* unexpectedly?
3. Why might you have to *step on it* in the morning? Does this happen often to you?
4. What was the last item you bought that you considered *a steal?* Where did you buy it?
5. Have you ever worked on something and *screwed* it *up?* How did you finally fix it?
6. Have you ever *goofed up* on an important test? Why did it happen?
7. Have you ever *gone off the deep end?* What happened?
8. For what reasons might an athlete *lose his or her touch* at a sport? Has this ever happened to you?
9. Is there any special skill that you have well *in hand?* What is it?
10. How much money do you have *on hand* right now?

L E S S O N 33

to kick (something) around: to discuss informally (over a period of time) (S) (also: **to toss around**)

○ At first my friends were reluctant to consider my suggestion, but they finally were willing to *kick* it *around* for a while.

○ Herb thought that we should *kick around* the idea of establishing a special fund for supporting needy members of the club.

on the ball: attentive, competent, alert

○ Jim was the only one who caught that serious error in the bookkeeping statements. He's really *on the ball*.

○ Ella was certainly *on the ball* when she remembered to reconfirm our flight arrangements. All the rest of us would have forgotten.

to make up: to meet or fulfill a missed obligation at a later time (**S**); to create, to invent (an idea) (**S**); to apply cosmetics to (**S**); to comprise, to be composed of
Note that all of the definitions are separable except the last one.

○ The teacher allowed several students who missed the exam to *make* it *up* during the next class.

○ The little boy *made up* a bad excuse for wearing his dirty shoes in the house, so his mother punished him.

○ Dee was able to *make* her face *up* in half the normal time because she didn't use much *makeup*.

○ Two separate bodies—the House of Representatives and the Senate—*make up* the Congress of the United States.

to make up with: to resolve differences with
This idiom is used for differences of opinion between friends and lovers.

○ Gundula *made up with* her roommate after their serious misunderstanding about arrangements for the party.

○ After the bad quarrel the two lovers kissed and *made up with* each other.

to pull together: to gather, to collect (information) (**S**); to gain control of one's emotions (**S**)
A reflexive pronoun must be used for the second definition.

○ The reporter *pulled together* information from several sources in preparing the newspaper article.

to give (someone) a break: to provide a person with another opportunity or chance (S); not to expect too much work from (S); not to expect someone to believe (S)

Command forms are most common with this idiom. For the third definition, the pronoun *me* must be used.

○ The driver pleaded with the police officer to *give* him *a break* and not issue him a ticket for speeding.

○ When the students heard how much homework the teacher wanted them to do over the holiday, they begged, "*Give* us *a break*, Professor Doyle!"

○ Oh, Jim, *give me a break!* That's a terrible excuse for being late.

to bow out: to stop doing as a regular activity, to remove oneself from a situation

The related idiom **to want out** indicates that someone desires to bow out.

○ She *bowed out* as the school's registrar after sixteen years of service.

○ One of the two partners *wanted out* of the deal because they couldn't agree on the terms of the contract.

EXERCISES

Substitute an idiomatic expression for the word or words in italics, making any necessary grammatical changes as well. Then complete each sentence appropriately with your own idea. Also try to use idioms from previous lessons.

1. At the amusement center, Sean was about to . . . when he *became afraid to do it.*

2. Leanne talked to her supervisor *directly* about . . .

3. The politician asked his friends if they *supported* him on . . .

4. Ted *fell in love with* the actress as soon as . . .

5. When Mrs. Garcia told her husband that their son . . . , Mr. Garcia responded, *"That seems likely."*

6. Joseph's roommate had been sick, so Joseph *gave* him *information* on . . .

7. I don't understand what *motivates* Diana *to behave that way*; she . . .

8. The boss *gave* his employee *another opportunity* when . . .

9. When the teacher told the students that . . . , the students said, *"Don't expect too much work from us!"*

10. One of the members of the committee *removed herself from the situation* because . . .

   Answer these questions orally by making use of the idiomatic expressions studied in this lesson.

1. Have you ever been about to do something important or dangerous, and then *gotten cold feet?* What was it?

2. Besides a car, what items can be *traded in* for new purchases? Have you ever *traded* something *in?* What was it?

3. Why might a student need to have a *face-to-face* talk with a teacher?

4. For what reasons might you not *be with it*? Are you *with it* today? Why or why not?

5. Have you ever *fallen for* someone who was deceiving you? How did you feel? How did you resolve the situation?

6. It's sometimes difficult to figure out what *makes* certain kinds of people *tick*. What kinds of people would you suggest?

7. In general, who would you feel compelled to *cover for*? Have you ever had to do this?

8. If you were a judge, under what condition might you give someone who had committed a serious crime *a break*?

9. What unbelievable statement might someone make that would cause you to respond, *"Give me a break!"*?

10. Why might you choose to *bow out* of a situation?

L E S S O N 35

to pin on: to find guilty of a crime or offense (S) (also: **to hang on**)
This idiom is divided by a noun phrase containing the crime or offense. The accused person is mentioned after the preposition on.

○ The prosecuting attorney tried to *pin* the murder *on* the victim's husband, but the jury returned a verdict of "not guilty."

○ I wasn't anywhere near the window when it got broken. You can't *pin* that *on* me.

to get a rise out of: to provoke a response from
This idiom is usually used when someone is teased into responding in anger or annoyance.

○ You can kid me all day about my mistake, but you won't *get a rise out of* me.

○ I *got a rise out of* Marvin when I teased him about his weight. Marvin weighs over two-hundred pounds.

to stick around: to stay or remain where one is, to wait
This idiom is used when someone is waiting for something to happen or for someone to arrive.

○ Todd had to *stick around* the house all day until the new furniture was finally delivered in the late afternoon.
○ Why don't you *stick around* for a while and see if Sarah eventually shows up?

to pick up the tab: to pay the cost or bill
This idiom applies when someone pays for the cost of another person's meal, tickets, etc.

○ The advertising manager is flying to Puerto Rico for a conference, and her firm is *picking up the tab*.
○ The government *picked up the tab* for the visiting dignitary. It paid for all of the lodging and meals, as well as transportation, during his stay.

by the way: incidentally
This idiom is used when someone thinks of something further in the course of a conversation.

○ Movies are my favorite form of entertainment. Oh, *by the way*, have you seen the new picture that's playing at the Bijou?
○ Vera's been divorced for three years now. She told me, *by the way*, that she never plans to remarry.

to go to town: to do something with enthusiasm and thoroughness

○ Our interior decorator really *went to town* in remodeling our living room. I'm afraid to ask how much it's going to cost.
○ Charlie really *went to town* on his research project. He consulted over forty reference works and wrote a ninety-page report.

to let slide: to neglect a duty (S); to ignore a situation (S)

- ○ Terry knew that she should have paid the electric bill on time instead of *letting* it *slide*. Now the utility company has turned off her service.
- ○ When he tried to get a rise out of me by mentioning my failure to receive a promotion at work, I just *let* it *slide*.

search me: I don't know (also: **beats me**)
This idiom is used informally, usually as a command form.

- ○ When Elmer asked his wife if she knew why the new neighbors left their garage door open all night, she responded, "*Search me.*"
- ○ When I asked Derek why his girlfriend wasn't at the party yet, he said, "*Beats me.* I expected her an hour ago."

to get off one's chest: to express one's true feelings (S)
This idiom is used when someone has long waited to express themselves.

- ○ Ellen felt a lot better when she finally talked to a counselor and *got* the problem *off her chest.*
- ○ Faye hasn't shared her concern about her marriage with her husband yet. I think that she should *get* it *off her chest* soon.

to live it up: to spend money freely, to live luxuriously

- ○ Kyle and Eric saved up money for two years so that they could travel to Europe and *live it up.*
- ○ After receiving a large inheritance from a rich aunt, I was able to *live it up* for years.

to liven up: to energize, to make more active (also: **to pick up**) (S)

- ○ The teacher occasionally took the class on field trips just to *liven* things *up* a bit.
- ○ The animals in the zoo began to *liven up* when evening came and the temperatures dropped.
- ○ Many people have to drink coffee every morning just to *pick* themselves *up.*

to have a voice in: to share involvement in

○ The new vice-president was promised that she would *have a voice in* developing the company's international expansion.

○ The students are trying to *have a voice in* college affairs by gaining representation on administrative committees.

Substitute an idiomatic expression for the word or words in italics, making any necessary grammatical changes as well. Then complete each sentence appropriately with your own idea. Also try to use idioms from previous lessons.

1. The police were successful in *finding* the criminal *guilty* of the robbery because . . .

2. My older brother is always able to *provoke a response from* me when he . . .

3. Why don't you *stay here* for a while longer? We're still . . .

4. The director *paid the bill* for the meal when he invited . . .

5. The neighbors really *did something with enthusiasm* when they worked together to . . .

6. I understand that Bill . . . because he *neglected his responsibilities* again and again.

7. In order to *express their true feelings about a problem,* some people . . .

8. On their honeymoon, the young couple *lived luxuriously* by . . .

9. In order to *energize* the party, the host and hostess . . .

10. The preferred candidate for the new position would not . . . until management agreed that she would *share involvement in* budget matters.

Answer these questions orally by making use of the idiomatic expressions studied in this lesson.

1. When you were a child, do you remember your brother, sister, or friend ever trying to *pin* something *on* you? What was it?

2. What kind of person is it easy to *get a rise out of?* What kind is it difficult to *get a rise out of?* Which are you?

3. If someone is late in meeting you, about how long would you *stick around* before leaving? Has this happened to you recently?

4. When was the last time that you *picked up the tab* for someone? Has anyone *picked up the tab* for you recently?

5. Are you the kind of person who is likely to make an issue out of a serious problem, or rather to *let it slide?* Why?

6. Can you think of a reason why the expression *search me* is used to mean *I don't know?* (In other words, why is the verb *search* used in this way?)

7. Why do people sometimes hold problems inside instead of *getting them off their chests* right away? Which approach are you most likely to take?

8. Have you ever had a chance *to live it up*? Describe what you did.

9. What are some different ways of *livening up* an event such as a wedding?

10. In a democracy, how do citizens of a country *have a voice in* government affairs?

L E S S O N 36

to check in: to register at a hotel or motel; to leave or deposit for transporting or safekeeping (S)
The adjective form *check-in* derives from this idiom.

○ Courtney arrived in town at mid-day and promptly-*checked in* at the Plaza Hotel. The hotel permitted an early *check-in* time.

○ There were dozens of people at the airline counters waiting to *check* their bags *in* for their flights.

to check out: to pay the bill at a hotel or motel and then leave; to investigate, to examine (S)
The adjective form *check-out* derives from this idiom.

○ The latest you should *check out* of the hotel is 12 noon. However, in your case, we can set a special *check-out* time of 2:00 P.M.

○ The police received a call from someone claiming to have witnessed a murder. The police sent two detectives to *check* the call *out* right away.

to take at one's word: to accept what one says as true, to believe

○ When he offered to be responsible for the fund raiser, I *took him at his word*. Now he's saying that he's not available to do it.

○ You should be careful about *taking her at her word.*
She's been known to say one thing but to do another.

to serve (the/one's) purpose: to be useful, to suit one's needs or requirements

○ I don't have a screwdriver to open this, but I think that a knife *will serve the purpose.*
○ Jane prefers working to studying, so it *served her purpose* to drop out of school and take that job.

in the worst way: very much, greatly

○ Jim and Claudia want to have children *in the worst way.* They are trying very hard to conceive.
○ Because Umer has relatives in Turkey, he wants to visit there *in the worst way.*

to cop out: to avoid one's responsibility, to quit
This idiom is an informal version of the second definition *to back out* (Lesson 29). The noun form **copout** means *an excuse for avoiding responsibility.*

○ Evelyn had agreed to help us with arrangements for the party, but she *copped out* at the last minute.
○ I can't believe that Cindy offered such an explanation for failing to show up. What a poor *copout!*

to line up: to form a line; to arrange to have, to manage to obtain (S)

○ The moviegoers *lined up* in front of the theater showing the most popular film of the summer.
○ Rob is going to schedule the famous author to speak at the convention if he can *line* her *up* in time.

to lose one's cool: to get excited, angry, or flustered

○ Despite the boos from some in the audience, the actors on stage never *lost their cool.*
○ Although the group of skiers were in danger from an apparent avalanche, their ski guide never *lost his cool.*

to leave open: to delay making a decision on (S)

○ In making up the job announcement, the firm decided to *leave* the salary *open* until a qualified candidate was found.

○ We know that the annual summer camp will be held in August, but let's *leave* the exact dates *open* for now.

to turn on: to interest greatly, to excite (S)
The idiom with the opposite meaning is **to turn off**. These idioms are used to form the nouns **turnon** and **turnoff**.

○ Does great art *turn* you *on*? I find going to a museum and viewing classic works of art a real *turnon*.

○ Going to a bar and having silly conversation with strangers really *turns* me *off*. In fact, most bar scenes are really *turnoffs* to me.

to miss the boat: to lose an opportunity, to fail in some undertaking

○ The precious metals market was looking up several months ago, but unfortunately most investors *missed the boat*.

○ Mr. Vlasic's new business went bankrupt within a short time. He really *missed the boat* by opening a tanning salon near the beach.

to think up: to invent, to create (also: **to dream up**)
This idiom is often used for an unusual or foolish thought.

○ Who *thought up* the idea of painting the living room walls bright red?

○ When asked by the teacher why she was late, the student *dreamed up* a plausible excuse.

EXERCISES

Substitute an idiomatic expression for the word or words in italics, making any necessary grammatical changes as well. Then complete each sentence appropriately with your own idea. Also try to use idioms from previous lessons.

1. The Smiths *registered* at the hotel as soon as . . .

2. The Smiths also *deposited* some jewelry at the front desk because . . .

3. The jealous husband hired a private detective to *investigate* the possibility that . . .

4. *I accepted what my financial advisor had to say* about . . .

5. On the Thursday before a three-day holiday weekend, it *suited the worker's needs* to . . .

6. While shopping in the expensive store, Mrs. Thurston . . . *very much.*

7. To ensure . . ., the politician *managed to obtain* the support of his colleagues in the Senate.

8. The athlete *got angry and flustered* on national television when . . .

9. We *delayed making a decision on* the arrangements for the wedding because . . .

10. Even though I had urged my parents to . . . , my parents *lost an opportunity* when the stock market . . .

Answer these questions orally by making use of the idiomatic expressions studied in this lesson.

1. What kind of items beside jewelry might a guest want to *check in* at the front desk of a hotel?

2. What is the latest that you have ever been able to *check out* of a hotel? Were you required to pay an extra fee for this arrangement?

3. If you and a friend are walking on a beach, what do you think your friend could mean if he or she says, "*Check that out!*"

4. Have you ever *taken someone at his or her word*, only to be disappointed at a later time? What happened?

5. What is it that you want at the present time *in the worst way*?

6. Have you ever *copped out* of a responsibility by *thinking up* a reasonable excuse? How do you feel when you do this? Why?

7. Think of different kinds of events or situations where people have to *line up.*

8. What kind of situation might cause you to *lose your cool*? Does this happen easily to you, or not?

9. Why might you *leave* arrangements for a trip *open*? Has this ever happened to you?

10. What kinds of sports or hobbies *turn* you *on*?

LESSON 37

to throw (someone) a curve: to introduce an unexpected topic, causing embarrassment (S)

○ The first week of class was going very well until a student *threw* the teacher *a curve* by suggesting that the textbook was too difficult.

○ The director asked us in advance to stick to the meeting agenda and not to *throw* him *any curves.*

to make waves: to create a disturbance, usually by complaining

This idiom is similar in meaning to the previous idiom, but the emphasis is on the aspect of complaining rather than causing embarrassment.

- ○ In most companies, an employee who *makes waves* is not appreciated.
- ○ The meeting was going smoothly until one of the participants *made waves* about the newly revised compensation package.

to carry on: to continue as before; to conduct, to engage in; to behave in an immature manner

- ○ Even in the face of disaster, the inhabitants *carried on* as though nothing had happened.
- ○ The business associates decided to *carry on* their discussion in the hotel bar instead of the conference room.
- ○ I can't believe that John *carried on* so much just because his dog died. He looked depressed and cried for weeks after it happened.

not on your life: absolutely not (also: **no way**)

This idiom is used as a kind of exclamation by itself.

- ○ You're asking me to invest in that poorly rated company just because you know the son of the president? *Not on your life!*
- ○ When a friend tried to get Mark to jump out of a plane with a parachute, he immediately responded, "*No way!*"

to cover ground: to be extensive, to discuss much material

Forms such as *a lot of, too much, too little* are used before the noun *ground*.

- ○ That national commission's report on urban ghettos *covers a lot of ground*. Many of the recommendations are too costly to implement.
- ○ In his first lecture on Greek philosophers, I thought that our professor *covered too little ground*.

to mind the store: to be responsible for an office while others are gone

- It seems that all of our employees are taking a lunch break at the same time. I wonder who's *minding the store*.
- Lynne agreed to *mind the store* while the others went outside to watch the parade passing by.

to throw the book at: to punish with full penalty, to be harsh on

- Because the criminal was a repeat offender, the judge *threw the book at* him with heavy fines and a long prison term.
- My boss *threw the book at* me when he discovered that I had been using company time for personal business. I was severely reprimanded and forced to make up the lost time.

to put one's foot in: to say or do the wrong thing
This idiom is used with the noun phrase *one's mouth* or the pronoun *it*.

- Fred really *put his foot in his mouth* when he called his supervisor by the wrong name.
- I really *put my foot in it* when I forgot my girlfriend's birthday and didn't buy her anything. She almost lost her cool.

to be up for grabs: to become available to others
This idiom is used when something is highly desirable to many other people.

- When one of the full-time contract instructors stepped down, her nice office overlooking the river *was up for grabs*.
- Did you know that Senator Stone is retiring and that her Senate seat *is up for grabs*?

to show off: to display one's ability in order to attract attention (S); to let others see, to expose to public view (S)
This idiom can form the noun **showoff** for the first definition.

- ○ Elizabeth is an excellent swimmer, but I don't like the way she *shows off* in front of everyone. It's very obvious that she enjoys being a *showoff.*
- ○ Jacquie *showed* her large wedding ring *off* to all her friends.

to learn the ropes: to become familiar with routine procedures at work or school

- ○ The job applicant didn't have much previous experience or knowledge, but she seemed intelligent enough to *learn the ropes* quickly.
- ○ It took the new schoolteacher a year to *learn the ropes* regarding administative and curricular matters.

to keep one's fingers crossed: to hope to have good results, to hope that nothing bad will happen
This idiom reflects the way people cross their fingers to hope for good luck.

- ○ Let's *keep our fingers crossed* that we got passing grades on that college entrance exam.
- ○ Jerry *kept his fingers crossed* that the good weather would hold up for the picnic he was planning for the coming weekend.

EXERCISES

Substitute an idiomatic expression for the word or words in italics, making any necessary grammatical changes as well. Then complete each sentence appropriately with your own idea. Also try to use idioms from previous lessons.

1. After discovering some improper contracts arranged by his company, a worker *created a disturbance by* . . .

2. The professor decided to *conduct* her class in the park because . . .

3. The teenager *behaved in an immature manner* for quite a while when his parents . . .

4. Martha answered, *"Absolutely not!"*, when her friend . . .

5. Because the instructor would *discuss too many matters* in the course, the student . . .

6. When the boss went out for lunch with some visitors, she asked . . . *to be responsible for the office.*

7. The judge *was harsh on* the defendant who . . .

8. The long-time manager's office suddenly *became available to others,* and many associates . . .

9. The excellent athlete *displayed his ability and attracted attention* at the regional track meet by . . .

10. It was difficult for . . . *to become familiar with the routine procedures* at the university.

Answer these questions orally by making use of the idiomatic expressions studied in this lesson.

1. Has anyone *thrown you a curve* recently? What happened?

2. When might a government worker decide to *make waves*? Have you heard or read of any instances of this recently?

3. Where is a common place to *carry on* a discussion? What less common places might a discussion be *carried on*?

4. Do you remember ever *carrying on* when you were a child? What did your parents do to stop you?

5. Do you like to take classes that *cover a lot of ground* or *cover little ground*? Why?

6. Would it ever be appropriate to *throw the book at* someone for *putting their foot in their mouth*? Why or why not?

7. Do you know anyone who likes to *show off*? What do they do?

8. Are you ever a *showoff*? When?

9. Suppose that you are interested in entering an unusual occupation such as that of a circus performer or magician. What would be the best way of *learning the ropes*?

10. Give an example of when you might *keep your fingers crossed*.

LESSON 38

to land on one's feet: to recover safely from an unpleasant or dangerous situation

○ After a series of personal and professional difficulties, it's amazing that George *has landed on his feet* so quickly.

○ Some young adults get into so much trouble at school that they are never able *to land on their feet* again. They drop out before graduating.

to dish out: to distribute in large quantity (**S**); to speak of others in a critical manner (**S**)

- ○ Mary's mom *dished out* two or three scoops of ice cream for each child at the birthday party.
- ○ Larry can't seem to take any criticism of his actions but he certainly likes to *dish it out.*

to get through to: to communicate with, to make someone understand (also: **to break through to**)
This idiom has the meaning of *to make someone "catch on"* (Lesson 29, eighth idiom, the first definition)

- ○ Some of the students in my reading class understand English so poorly that it is difficult to *get through to* them.
- ○ The doctors have never succeeded in *breaking through to* Mr. Ames, who is a silent and secretive patient.

to keep one's word: to fulfill a promise, to be responsible
An idiom with the opposite meaning is **to break one's word.**

- ○ Suzanne *kept her word* to me not to let on to others that I intend to step down next month.
- ○ Thomas always intends to *keep his word*, but invariably the end result is that he *breaks his word.* He just isn't capable of being a responsible person.

to be over one's head: to be very busy, to have too much to do (also: **to be up to one's ears**); to be beyond one's ability to understand

- ○ I'd love to take a week off for a hiking trip, but at the moment I *am over my head* in work. Maybe next week when I'm only *up to my ears!*
- ○ It was impossible for the tutor to get through to Bill about the physics problem because the subject matter was *over Bill's head.*

to ask for: to deserve, to receive a just punishment (also: **to bring upon**)

- ○ If you drink alcohol and then drive a car, you're only *asking for* trouble.
- ○ Don't complain about your cut in salary. You *asked for* it by refusing to heed our repeated warnings not to be late and inefficient.

to be a far cry from: to be very different from

- ○ I enjoyed visiting Seattle, but it *was a far cry from* the ideal vacation spot I expected.
- ○ Ned is enjoying his new job, but his responsibilities *are a far cry from* what he was told they would be.

by all means: certainly, definitely, naturally (also: **of course**); using any possible way or method

- ○ If the Johnsons invite us for dinner, then *by all means* we have to return the invitation. *Of course*, we don't have to invite their children, too.
- ○ In order to ensure its survival, the ailing company has to obtain an infusion of cash *by all means*.

to get out from under: to restore one's financial security, to resolve a difficult financial obligation

- ○ After years of struggling to get ahead, the young couple finally *got out from under* their debts.
- ○ The ailing company, succeeding in obtaining the necessary cash, was able *to get out from under* its financial burdens.

to take the bull by the horns: to handle a difficult situation with determination
This idiom is usually used when someone has been postponing an action for some time and finally wants or needs to resolve it.

- ○ After three years of faithful service, Jake decided to *take the bull by the horns* and ask his boss for a raise.
- ○ Vic has been engaged to Laura for a long time now, and I know that he loves her. He should *take the bull by the horns* and ask her to marry him.

to give (someone) a hand: to assist, to aid, to help (also: **to lend someone a hand**) (S)

- ○ Would you *give* me *a hand* lifting this heavy box?
- ○ When Terry's car broke down at night on the highway, no one would stop to *lend* her *a hand*.

to give (someone) a big hand: to clap one's hands in applause, to applaud (S)

○ After the talented new vocalist had sung her number, the audience *gave* her *a big hand*.

○ Should we *give a big hand* to each beauty contestant is as she is introduced, or should we wait until all the introductions are finished?

Substitute an idiomatic expression for the word or words in italics, making any necessary grammatical changes as well. Then complete each sentence appropriately with your own idea. Also try to use idioms from previous lessons.

1. It took some time for the artist to *recover from the difficult situation* . . .

2. Billy's mother *distributed in large quantity* . . . to all the kids at the birthday party.

3. When parents are having trouble *communicating with* their children, they can . . .

4. When I decided to change apartments, my friend *fulfilled her promise* about . . .

5. Larry *has too much to do* at work because . . .

6. The child running on the wet pavement beside the swimming pool *deserved it* when . . .

to get out of line: to disobey or ignore normal procedures or rules (also: **to step out of line**)

○ When a child *gets out of line* in that teacher's class, she uses the old-fashioned method of making the child sit in the corner of the room.

○ Any employee who *steps out of line* by coming to work in an unacceptable condition will be fired.

dry run: rehearsal, practice session

○ The college president requested a *dry run* of the graduation ceremony in order to ensure that all aspects went smoothly.

○ Before the manager presented the reorganizational plans to the board of directors, he did several *dry runs* of his presentation.

to play by ear: to play music that one has heard but never read (**S**); to proceed without plan, to do spontaneously (**S**) The pronoun *it* is often used with the second definition.

○ That pianist can play most popular music *by ear*. She never needs to read sheet music.

○ My husband wanted to plan our trip carefully, but I argued that it was more fun if we *played* it *by ear*.

to be in (someone's) shoes: to be in another person's position, to face the same situation as another person

○ If I *were in your shoes*, I wouldn't take too many classes this semester.

○ When his boss finds out about that accounting error, I wouldn't want to *be in his shoes*.

to keep after: to remind constantly, to nag

○ Lynn always has *to keep after* her children about cleaning up their rooms and doing chores around the house.

○ Lon is so forgetful that it's necessary to *keep after* him about every little thing.

to fix up: to repair or put back in good condition (S); to arrange a date or an engagement for another person (S)

- ○ Instead of buying an expensive new home, we decided to buy an older home and *fix* it *up* ourselves.
- ○ Since my visiting friend didn't have a date for dinner, I *fixed* her *up* with a male friend of mine. They got along very well together.

to be had: to be victimized or cheated

- ○ When the jeweler confirmed that the diamonds that the woman had purchased abroad were really fake, she exclaimed, *"I've been had!"*
- ○ The angry customer complained about being overcharged at the store, asserting that this was the third time that he *had been had.*

Substitute an idiomatic expression for the word or words in italics, making any necessary grammatical changes as well. Then complete each sentence appropriately with your own idea. Also try to use idioms from previous lessons.

1. Because most of her elementary school students *were wasting time,* the teacher . . .

2. When Joey *spoke disrespectfully to* his mother, she . . .

3. When he learned that the owner *wasn't available,* the visiting salesperson . . .

4. Greg is willing to help his brother with some household chores, but he *refuses to consider* . . .

5. If you *disobey the rules* one more time, I will . . .

6. The theater group did a *rehearsal* of the play before . . .

7. Mrs. Dixson has the special ability *to play* music *she has heard but never read.* She doesn't have to . . .

8. I wouldn't want *to be in Ted's position.* The police have discovered that he . . .

9. Every day after school, Harriet's parents have *to nag* her to . . .

10. I decided to *arrange an engagement for* him because he . . .

Answer these questions orally by making use of the idiomatic expressions studied in this lesson.

1. Are you usually a serious person, or do you like to *goof off* a lot? Why might *goofing off* sometimes be healthy for you?
2. When you were young, did you *talk back to* your parents? Why or why not?
3. Do you pay attention to whether clothing fashions *are in* or *out*? What is an advantage of not paying attention?
4. Suppose that your boss sometimes asks you to stay late at the office and do extra work for him. At what point would you *draw the line* and refuse?
5. What happens to an athlete who *gets out of line* during a sporting event such as baseball or international football ("soccer" in the United States)?

6. If you had to give a speech in class, would you do *a dry run*? Why or why not?

7. When you travel, do you like to plan your trip carefully or to *play* it *by ear*?

8. When you were young, what did your parents have to *keep after* you about? Did you ever learn to remember it, or do you still forget?

9. Have you ever *fixed* someone *up* with a date, or have you ever been *fixed up* with a date yourself? Can you imagine why the term *blind date* is sometimes used in such cases?

10. Have you ever *been had* by someone you just met, such as a store clerk or a stranger on the street? What happened?

A. Match the idiom in the left column with the definition in the right column.

___	1. let alone	a. I don't know
___	2. on the ball	b. certainly, definitely
___	3. search me	c. nervous, irritable
___	4. by the way	d. rehearsal, practice session
___	5. on hand	e. and certainly not
___	6. by all means	f. incidentally
___	7. more or less	g. available, nearby
___	8. a steal	h. in general
___	9. dry run	i. attentive, alert
___	10. on the whole	j. directly, personally
___	11. on edge	k. approximately, almost
___	12. face-to-face	l. very inexpensive

B. In the space provided, mark whether each sentence is true (**T**) or false (**F**).

1. If you have succeeded in *landing on your feet* after financial difficulties, things probably *are looking up* in your life. _____

2. If you *go through channels* in submitting a complaint, you are probably *making waves* in your company. _____

3. If someone asks why you did something and you can't *think up* a good reason, you might respond, "*Search me.*" _____

4. If you know someone who likes to *put* others *on*, you can usually *take* that person *at their word.* _____

5. If the subject matter of an academic field often *is over your head*, you may not *be cut out for* that field. _____

6. Parents might *go off the deep end* if they have *to wait up for* their child very late without knowing what he or she *is up to*. _____

7. If you get a problem *off your chest*, you are *beating around the bush*. _____

8. If you are able to *get through to* someone, you have *wasted your breath*. _____

9. If you *are* not with someone while they are explaining something, you *are catching on*. _____

10. You might *back out* of an activity that could cause you *to get cold feet* at the last minute. _____

11. If you dislike *playing* something *by ear*, you will probably *leave* it *open*. _____

12. If you are *learning the ropes*, it is possible that you might *goof up* once in a while. _____

C. Fill in each blank with the appropriate form of the idioms using *give* listed below. Some expressions come from Lessons 1 to 27.

give and take	to give up	to give in
to give off	to give out	to give one a break
to give birthto	to give one a hand	to give one a big hand

1. Mrs. Johnson was very surprised when she _____ twin boys.

2. Because it was the first time that I had fooled around in class, I asked the teacher _____.

3. A successful marriage is mostly a matter of _____ between husband and wife.

4. This box is too heavy for me to lift alone. Could you _____?

5. The lecturer was so interesting that the audience _____ at the end of the talk.

6. The man stood on the street corner and _____ advertising flyers to the people passing by.

7. Could you please take this garbage outside? It _____ a very bad smell.

8. The army forces _____ when they discovered that they were surrounded by the enemy.

9. I usually don't _____ so easily, but this work is too hard for me to do.

D. Fill in each blank with the appropriate form of the idioms using keep listed below. Some expressions come from Lessons 1-27.

to keep one's head	to keep with	to keep in touch with
to keep one's word	to keep after	to keep in mind
to keep track of	to keep away	to keep one's fingers crossed

1. In the emergency situation, Alex was able _____ and save the child from drowning in the ocean.

2. At the racetrack, none of the horses were able _____ the horse that was expected to win the race.

3. When we visited Disneyland, we had to be careful _____ our children in the large crowds of people.

4. You have _____ Tanya to return the type-writer or she will forget time and again.

5. You should _____ about doing that important task and not neglect to attend to it any longer.

6. Even though you're moving to another city, we should _____ each other as much as possible.

7. While I was cooking with hot grease on the stove, I warned others _____ in order not to get burned.

8. When teaching beginning-level English students, it is important _____ that their range of vocabulary is quite limited.

9. The weather forecast is calling for cloudy skies tomorrow. We should _____ that it doesn't rain during the picnic.

E. Fill in each blank with the appropriate form of the idioms using *go* listed below. Some expressions come from Lessons 1 to 27.

to go through	to go to town	to go without saying
touch and go	to go in for	to go around
to go over	to go off	to go with

1. I was too tired to get up in the morning when my alarm clock _____, so I turned it off and went back to sleep.

2. My presentation to the class _____ so well that the students gave me a big hand.

3. The delicate operation was _____ for several hours, but finally the surgeons were able to finish successfully.

4. We just went to the store an hour ago to buy more beer, and already there isn't enough _____.

5. I can't understand how we _____ so much beer in such a short time.

6. When we remodeled our house, we added a master bedroom, a large bathroom with jacuzzi, and a walk-in closet. We really _____.

7. I really enjoy playing chess. Do you _____ playing chess as well?

8. That you should stay home if you are very sick _____.

9. Do you think that this grey shirt _____ these beige pants?

Appendix

Lesson 1

English	Spanish	French	German
get on	subirse, montarse	monter	einsteigen
get off	bajarse, apearse	descendre, sortir	aussteigen
put on	ponerse	mettre	aufsetzen, anziehen
take off	quitarse	enlever	ausziehen
call up	llamar (por teléfono)	téléphoner, un coup de fil	anrufen
turn on	encender, abrir	allumer, ouvrir	anmachen, andrehen
turn off	apagar, cerrar	éteindre, fermer	ausmachen, ausdrehen
right away	inmediatamente	immédiatement	sofort
pick up	tomar, coger	ramasser, prendre	aufheben
sooner or later	tarde o temprano	inévitablement	früher oder später
get up	levantarse	se lever	aufstehen
at first	al principio	au premier abord	zuerst

Lesson 2

English	Spanish	French	German
dress up	emperifollarse	s'habiller, se mettre'en Grande toilette	schönes Gewand anziehen
at last	por fin	enfin	endlich
as usual	como de costumbre	comme d'habitude	wie gewöhn-lich

English	Spanish	French	German
find out	averiguar	trouver, découvrir	feststellen,
look at	mirar, contemplar	regarder, envisager	ansehen, anschauen
look for	buscar, indagar	chercher, rechercher	suchen
all right	satisfactorio, afirmativo	c'est bien	zufrieden sein, richtig
all along	desde el principio	depuis le debut	schon immer, von Beginweg
little by little	poco a poco, lentamente	au fur et à mesure	nach und nach
tire out	exhaustar, agotar	n'en pouvoir plus	übermüdet
call on	acudir a, visitar	visiter	esuchen
never mind	no se preocupe, no importa	peu importe	schon gug

Lesson 3

English	Spanish	French	German
pick out	seleccionar, escoger	choisir	aussuchen
take one's time	tomarse su tiempo, proceder con calma	prendre son temps	Zeit nehmen
talk over	discutir	discuter	besprechen
lie down	acostarse	s'étendre	sich hinlegen
stand up	ponerse de pie	se mettre debout	aufstehen
sit down	sentarse	s'asseoir	sich hinsetzen
all day long	todo el día	toute la journée	den ganzen Tag
by oneself	por sí mismo, solo	tout seul	alleine
on purpose	a propósito, adrede	exprès	absichtlich

get along with	llevarse bien o mal (con), irle bien	s'entendre, faire de progrès avec	auskommen
make a difference	ser importante, importarle	être important	keinen Unter- schied machen
take out	sacar, extraer	sortir	herausnehmen

Lesson 4

take part in	tomar parte, participar	participer à	teilnehemen
at all	de ninguna manera	du tout	überhaupt nicht
look up	indagar, buscar	chercher	nachschauen
wait on	despachar, servir	servir	bedienen
at least	por lo menos	au moins	wenigstens
so far	hasta ahora	jusqu'ici	bis jetzt
take a walk	dar un paseo a pie	faire une promenade	Spaziergang machen
take a trip	hacer un viaje	faire un voyage	Reise unterne- hmen
try on	probarse	essayer	anprobieren
think over	reflexionar	réfléchir	überlegen
take place	suceder, ocurrir	avoir lieu	stattfinden
put away	guardar, recoger	ranger	weglegen

Lesson 5

look out	tener cuidado	faire attention	vorsicht, sich vorsehen
shake hands	dar la mano	serrer la main	sich die Hände geben
get back	regresar	revenir, retourner	zurückkommen
catch cold	resfriarse, acatarrarse	prendre froid	sich erkälten

English	Spanish	French	German
get over	reponerse, restablecerse	se consoler, se remettre	hinwegkommen
make up one's mind	decidirse	se décider	sich entsch-liessen
change one's mind	cambiar de opinión o idea	changer d'idée, changer d'avis	Meinung ändern
for the time being	por ahora, mientras tanto	pour le moment	zur Zeit
for good	para siempre, permanentemente	pour de bon	für inmer, ständig
call off	cancelar	annuler	absagen
put off	posponer	ajourner	aufschieben
in a hurry	rápidamente	être pressé	in Eile

Lesson 6

English	Spanish	French	German
under the weather	no sentirse bien	être malade	sich unwohl fühlen, Krank sein
hang up	colgar	suspendre, raccrocher (téléphone)	aufhängen
count on	contar con	compter sur	rechnen auf
make friends	hacer amigos	faire des amis	Freundschaft anschliessen
out of order	descompuesto	ne pas fonctionner	ausser Betrieb
get to	llegar a	arriver à	ankommen
few and far between	infrecuente	rare	selten
look over	revisar, examinar	examiner, vérifier	prüfen, nachsehen
have time off	tener tiempo libre	avoir du temps libre	frei haben
go on	continuar	continuer à	fortfahren

put out	sofocar, apagar, extinguir	éteindre	auslöschen, ausmachen
all of a sudden	súbitamente, repentinamente, de pronto	tout à coup	plötzlich

Lesson 7

point out	señalar, mostrar	signaler, montrer du doigt	bezeichnen, anmerken
be up	terminar, llegar la hora	être terminé	beenden
be over	haber terminado	être fini	vorüber sein
on time	a la hora indicada	à l'heure, à temps	pünktlich sein
in time to	a tiempo, antes de la hora indicada	à temps	zur Zeit
get better	mejorar	aller mieux, s'améliorer	besser werden
get sick	enfermarse	tomber malade	krank werden
had better	es mejor que	il vaut mieux que	für besser halten
would rather	preferir	préférer	vorzichen
call it a day	parar de trabajar	finir la journée	Feirabend machen
figure out	resolver, entender	résoudre, comprendre	herausfinden; verstehen
think of	opinar de	penser à	hoch einschätzen

Lesson 8

be about to	estar a punto de	être sur le point de	im Begriff sein
turn around	dar la vuelta, cambiar totalmente	se retourner faire un virage total	umdrehen
take turns	alternar	alterner	abwechseln
pay attention	prestar atención	faire attention	aufpassen

English	Spanish	French	German
brush up on	refrescar, pulir	repasser	auffrischen
over and over	repetidamente	sans cesse	inmer wieder
wear out	gastarse	user	abgetragen, abgenutzt
throw away	botar, echar	jeter	wegwerfen
fall in love	enamorarse	tomber amoureux	sich verlieben
go out	cesar, apagarse, salir	sortir, cesser, s'eteindre	ausgehen
out of the question	imposible	impossible	unmöglich
have to do with	tener que ver con	y être pour quelque chose	zu tun haben mit

Lesson 9

English	Spanish	French	German
wake up	despertarse	s'éveiller, se réveiller	aufwachen
be in charge of	estar a cargo de	être chargé de	Sorge tragen fur
as soon as	tan pronto como	aussitôt que	so bald als
get in touch with	comunicarse con	communiquer avec	in Verbindung treten
have a good time	divertirse	bien s'amuser	sich amüsieren
in no time	rápidamente	tout de suite	innert Kürze
cut down on	reducir	reduire	einschränken
quite a few	muchos	pas mal de	einige
used to	acostumbraba, solia	avoir l'habitude de	fruher gewohnt sein an
be used to	estar acostumbrado a	être accoutumé a, avoir l'habitude de	Angewohnheit haben

get used to	acostumbrarse a	s'accoutumer à	sich einstellen auf
back and forth	de un lado a otro	va-et-vient	hin und her

Lesson 10

make sure	asegurar, garantizar	s'assurer de	sicher machen
now and then	de vez en cuando	de temps en temps	von Zeit zu Zeit
get rid of	deshacerse de	se défaire de, se débarasser de	loswerden
every other	cada dos	tous les deux	einen um den andern
go with	hacer juego, ir con, salir con	s'accorder, fréquenter, sortir avec	mitgehen, zusammen ausgehen
first-rate	primera clase, excelente	de première classe	erst Klassisch
come from	proceder de, ser oriundo de	venir de (quelque part)	herkommen
make good time	viajar rápidamente	voyager vite, bien marcher (train)	schnelle Fahrt haben
mix up	equivocar, mezclar, confundir	mélanger, s'embrouiller	durcheinander bringen
see about	ocuparse de	s'occuper de	nachsehen
make out	irle bien, salir bien	réussir	Erfolg haben
by heart	de memoria	par coeur	auswendig

Lesson 11

keep out	no entrar	défendre d'entrer	fernhalten
keep away	mantener distancia de, evitar	eviter	vermeiden
find fault with	criticar	trouver a redire	kritisieren

English	Spanish	French	German
be up to	depender de alguien, tener entre manos	dépendre de	abhängen von, machen
ill at ease	incómodo	peu confortable	unwohlfühlen
do over	volver a hacer	refaire	wiederholen
look into	investigar	examiner attentivement	prüfen
take hold of	agarrarse de	saisir	anfassen
get through	terminar, acabar	terminer	beenden
from now on	de ahora en adelante	a partir de ce moment	von nun an
keep track of	llevar cuenta de	enregistrer, tenir un registre	aufzeichnen, aufschreien
be (get) carried away	dejarse llevar, excederse	se laisser emporter	überreagieren

Lesson 12

English	Spanish	French	German
up to date	moderno, al día, al corriente	au courant, à la page	neuzeitlich, al corriente
out of date	anticuado, antiquo, arcaico	démodé, périmé, dépassé	ausser Mode
blow up	inflar, explotar, volar	gonfler, faire sauter, exploser	aufblasen, explodieren
catch fire	incendiarse	prendre feu	in Flammen ausbrechen
burn down	quemarse (un edificio)	détruire par le feu	abbrennen
burn up	quemar (se) completamente, enojarse	brûler entièrement, se fâcher	verbrennen, zornig machen
burn out	fundirse	brûler	ausbrennen
make good	tener éxito	réussir	Erfolg haben
stands to reason	ser natural, lógico	il va sans dire	ohne Zweifel

break out	estallar, comenzar sú- bitamente	éclater	ausbrechen
as for	en cuanto a	en tant que, quant à	was anbetrifft
feel sorry for	tener lástima de	avoir pitié de	Mitleid haben

Lesson 13

break down	romperse	ne plus marcher	versagen
turn out	resultar, acudir	finalement devenir, se presenter	herausdrehen, besuch
once in a blue moon	rara vez	une fois par hasard	selten
give up	dejar de, rendirse	se rendre, abdiquer, abandonner	aufgeben, passieren
cross out	tachar	barrer	durchstreichen
take for granted	presumir, tomar por descontado	présumer, tenir pour certain	für Selbstver- ständlich annehmen
take into account	tomar en cuenta, tener en consi- deración	tenir compte de	in Betracht ziehen
make clear	aclarar	clarifier	erklären
clear-cut	bien claro	net	ganz Klar
have on	tener puesto	porter	tragen
come to	volver en sí ascender, llegar a	revenir à soi, s 'élever	zu sich kom- men
call for	requerir, recomendar	nécessiter, recommander	fordern, dringen auf

Lesson 14

eat in/eat out	comer en casa/ comer fuera	manger à la maison/au restaurant	zu Hause essen, ausessen
cut and dried	predecible	simple	absehbar
look after	cuidar de	s'occuper de	aufpassen

English	Spanish	French	German
feel like	tener ganas de	avoir envie de	Lust haben
once and for all	de una vez y para siempre	une fois pour toutes	endgültig
hear from	recibir noticias de	recevoir des nouvelles	Nachricht bekommen
hear of	oír hablar de, saber de, considerar	entendre parler de, considérer	etwas hören von, über
make fun of	burlarse de	se moquer de, se rire de	sich lustig machen
come true	resultar cierto	devenir un fait accompli	wahr werden
as a matter of fact	en realidad, es más	le fait est que	tatsächlich Kopf gehen
have one's way	salirse con la suya	en faire à sa tête	mit Freude oder Ungeduld
look forward to	aguardar con ansia	attendre avec impatience	nach dem eigenen

Lesson 15

English	Spanish	French	German
inside out	al revés	dessous	Innenseite nach aussen
upside down	boca abajo	sens dessus	drunter und drüber verkehrt
fill in	rellenar espacio(s), informar	remplir, informer	Lücke aus fullen benachrichti gen
fill out	completar una planilla	remplir	ausfüllen
take advantage of	aprovecharse de	profiter de	ausnutzen
no matter	no importa	n'importe	ohne auf etwas zu achten

take up	estudiar, ocupar	étudier, occuper	studieren, belegen, ein- nehmen
take up with	consultar con	discuter avec	besprechen
take after	salir a	tenir de	sich ähnlich sein
in the long run	a la larga	à la longue	zum Schluss, am Ende
in touch	en comunicación	rester en contact	in Kontaktblei- ben
out of touch	sin comunicación, desligado	avoir perdu le contact avec	nicht auf dem Laufenden sein

Lesson 16

on one's toes	alerta	alerte	aufmerksam
get along	llevarse bien, irle bien (o mal)	s'entendre, se débrouiller	weiterkomen
hard of hearing	medio sordo	sourd d'oreille	schlecht hörig sein
see eye to eye	estar de acuerdo	être d'accord sur tous les points	einverstanden sein
have in mind	tener en mente, proponerse	avoir quelque chose à l'ésprit	im Sinn haben
keep in mind	recordar	se rappeler de	nicht vergessen
for once	al fin, sólo una vez	pour une fois	für ein undalle mal
go off	disparar, explotar partir	partir s'en aller	losgehen
grow out of	quitársele, dar origen	passer, naissance	auswachsen, Sache machen
make the best of	sacar el mejor partido posible	tirer le meilleur parti de	das Beste aus etwas machen

English	Spanish	French	German
cut off	cortar	couper, interrompre	abschneiden
cut out	recortar, cesar	découper, cesser de	ausschneiden, anhalten

Lesson 17

English	Spanish	French	German
blow out	reventarse, apagar (soplando)	avoir une crevaison, e'teindre, souffler	platzen, explodieren, auslöschen
become of	hacerse de, sucederle	se faire de	geworden aus, geschehen, passieren
shut up	cerrar, callarse	mettre les verrous, se taire	abschliessen, Mund halten
have got	tener, poseer	avoir	bekommen, besitzen
have got to (do something)	tener que hacer algo	devoir	etwas tun müssen
keep up with	mantenerse a la par de	aller aussi vite que	Schritt halten
on the other hand	sin embargo	d'autre part	hingegen jedoch
turn down	bajar, reducir, rechazar	baisser, refuser	schwächer stellen, ablehnen
fifty-fifty	a la mitad	moitié-moitié	fünfzig zu fünfzig
break in	estrenar, ajustar, interrumpir	assouplir, interrompre	eintragen, unterbrechen
a lost cause	causa perdida, inútil	une cause sans espoir	eineverlorene Angelegenheit
above all	sobre todo	par-dessus tout	hauptsächlich, über alles

Lesson 18

do without	prescindir de	se passer de	ohne etwas
according to	de acuerdo con, según	selon	gemäss, laut
be bound to	ser inevitable	être certain de	aufpassen
for sure	con seguridad	vraiment	ziemlich sicher
take for	tomar a uno por	prendre quelqu'un pour	hingehen, hinfahren
try out	probar	essayer	jemanden halten für
tear down	derribar, demoler	démolir	ausprobieren
tear up	rasgar, lacerar	déchirer	abreissen
go over (well)	ser apreciado	passer bien	schätzen
run out of	acabarse	manquer de	augehen
at heart	fundamentalmente	au fond	grundsätzlich
about to	a punto de	être sur le point de faire	soeben

Lesson 19

bite off	aceptar una responsabilidad excesiva	viser trop haut	mehr annehmen alsman ver Kraften kann
tell apart	distinguir entre	distinguer entre	unterschiden
all in all	teniendo todo en consideración	tour comptes faits	im ganzen
pass out	distribuir, repartir, desmayarse	répartir perdre conscience	verteilen, stockbesaffen
go around	alcanzar para todos, circular	suffire à tout le monde, circuler	herumgehen, herumreichen umlaufer
be in the way	estorbar	être de trop	im Wege sein
put on	ganar peso, representar	augmenter de poids, répresenter	zunehmen, auffüchren

English	Spanish	French	German
put up	construir, edificar levantar	construire, ériger lever	errichten, aufbauen, heben
put up with	tolerar, soportar	tolérer	ertragen, aushalten
in vain	en vano	en vain	vergeblich, vergebens
day in, and day out	a diario, día tras día	à longueur de journée	Tag ein und Tag aus
catch up	alcanzar	se rattraper	nachholen ein holen

Lesson 20

hold still	estarse quieto	rester tranquille	stillhalten
know by sight	conocer de vista	connaître de vue	von Ansehen kennen
be the matter	pasar algo	rien de dérégle, y avoir quelque chose	etwas nicht in Ordnung sein
bring up	criar, presentar	élever	erziehen
get lost	perderse	se perdre	sich verirren
hold up	durar, demorar	retarder, durer	verzögern dauern
run away	huir, escaparse	se sauver, s'échapper	weglaufen, wegrennen
rule out	descartar	eliminer	ausschliessen
by far	claramente	de loin, de beaucoup	bei weitem
see off	despedirse de alguien	voir partir quelqu'un	Abschied, nehmen
see out	acompañar a la salida	raccompagner à la porte	hinaus beglei- ten
no wonder	no extrañar	n'avoir rien d'éttonant	Kein Wunder

Lesson 21

go up	ir hasta, llegar hasta	conduire à, aller à, courir à	hinfahren, hinlaufen hingehen
go up to	dirigirse a	s'approcher de	entgegen gehen
hand in	presentar, entregar	remettre, donner	einreichen
in case	por si acaso	au cas où	in Falle
take apart	desarmar	démonter	ausein andernehmen
put together	armar	assembler	zusammen set-zen
be better off	irle mejor	valoir mieux	besser dran sein
be well-off	ser acomodado, tener dinero	dans l'aisance	vermögend sein
take by surprise	sorprender a alguien	prendre au dépourvu	überraschen
keep in touch with	mantenerse en contacto con	continuer à communiquer	in Verbindung bleiben
name after	darle el nombre de	être nommé d'après	nach jeman-den, ben-nant sein
hold on	agarrarse de, aguantar	s'accrocher à, attendez	sich festhalten dranbleiben

Lesson 22

stop by	visitar	s'arrêter en passant	an halten
drop a line	escribirle unas líneas a alguien	écrire un mot	jemandem ein par Worte schreiben
come across	encontrarse con dar la impresión	trouver par hasard, sembler	treffen, herausfinden, scheinen

English	Spanish	French	German
stand for	representar, aguantar a, tolerar	répresenter, tolérer	darstellen, sich gefallen lassen
stand a chance	tener probabilidad	avoir la chance de	eine Möglich-keit haben
take pains	esmerarse	prendre de la peine	etwas sorgfäl-tig tun, sich Mühe geben
look on	observar	regarder	beobachten
look up to	admirar	avoir un grand respect pour	bewundern, respektieren
look down on	depreciar	regarder de haut en bas	herabsehen auf
take off	despegar	décoller	abfliegen (abhauen)
pull off	lograr, detener el coche en la carretera	réussir, arrêter l'auto	fertigbringen, halten (auto)
keep (good) time	andar bien (un reloj)	être a l'heure	genau gehen

Lesson 23

English	Spanish	French	German
make do	improvisar	se débrouiller	auskommen
give birth to	dar a luz	donner naissance à, mettre au monde	zur Welt bringen
close call	librarse por los pelos	l'échapper elle	umein Haar
get on one's nerves	ponerlo a uno nervioso	porter sur les nerfs	nervös machen, auf die Nerven gehen
put down	dominar, reprimir, criticar injusta-mente	réprimer, critiquer injustemente	niederwerfen, niederdrucken kritisieren

go for	venderse por (precio), aspirar a	se vendre à, essayer d'obtenir	wert sein, anstreben
go in for	ser aficionado a	s'adonner à	etwas gern haben, Freude daran haben
stay up	acostarse tarde	veiller	aufbleiben
stay in	quedarse en casa	rester à la maison	zu Hause bleien
take over	encargarse de tomar or hacer otra vez	se charger de faire, prendre de nouveau	ubernehmen noch einmal machen
show up	presentarse, aparecerse, ser hallado	se présenter être trouvé	sich zeigen begründen
clean out	limpiar	nettoyer (à fond)	sauber machen, reinigen

Lesson 24

knock out	hacer perder el sentido de un golpe	faire perdre connaissance par un coup	jemanden bewusstlos machen, niederwerfen
knock oneself out	matarse del esfuerzo	se défoncer, se crever pour	sich überanstrengen
carry out	llevar a cabo	exécuter	ausführen
run into	encontrarse con	recontrer par hasard	unerwartet treffen
set out	salir a, exponer	se mettre en chemin	losgehen, ausstellen
set out to	emprender	se mettre à	sich vornehmen
draw up	trazar, preparar	tracer, preparer	zeichnen, ausfüllen
give and take	hacer concesiones	s'accommoder	entgegen kommen

English	Spanish	French	German
drop out of	dejar de asistir	quitter	verlassen
believe in	creer en	croire à	glauben an
cheer up	alegrarse, animarse	rendre courage, réjouir	aufmuntern
make sense	ser razonable, tener sentido	être logique	verständig sein

Lesson 25

English	Spanish	French	German
burst out crying/laughing	salir súbitamente, romper a llorar romper a reír	sortir en trombe eclater en sanglots, éclater de rire	hervorbrechen zu weinen anfangen, zu lachen
get away	escapar, huir	s'échapper, s'énfuir	loskommen
get away with	salirse con la suya	s'en tirer	mit etwas wegkommen
serve (someone right	merecer	mériter	recht geschehen
keep up	impedir el sueño, mantener el mismo paso	empêcher de dormir, continuer au même pas	beibehalten
keep up with	estar al día, entender	être au courant, suivre	schritthalten
stand out	sobresalir	se distinguer	auffallend sein, hervostehen
let on	dejar entrever, revelar	reveler à	wissen lassen
go wrong	salir mal	marcher mal, pas marcher	falsch gehen
meet (someone) halfway	llegar a un acuerdo	faire des concessions	auf halbem Wege treffen
check up on	revisar, comprobar	vérifier, examiner	nachprüfen, untersuchen
stick up	sobresalir	ressortir	herausstecken

Lesson 26

come about	suceder, ocurrir	se produire	sich ereignen
bring about	causar	causer, provoquer	verursachen
build up	aumentar	se fortifier, renforcer	auffrischen, aufbauen
die down	acabarse, apagarse	se calmer, s'éteindre	nechlassen, verringern
fade away	desaparecer poco a poco	décoître peu à peu	abklingen
die out	desaparecer	disparaître	aussterben
make out	descifrar, entender escribir	déchiffrer, écrire	ausschreiben, entziffern
live up to	cumplir, realizar	être à la hauteur de	erreichen, erfüllen
stick to	defender, mantener firme	persévérer	aushalten, beharren
stick it to	engañar, estafar	tromper, voler	übers Ohr hauen, begaunern
stand up for	salir en defensa de	défendre	eintreten für, sich einsetzen
cut corners	economizar	réuire (Réduire) les dépenses	sparsam wirtschaften

Lesson 27

take on	emplear, responsabilizarse	employer, engager	einstellen, engagieren
take down	descolgar, bajar, tomar nota de	décrocher, prendre note de	herunternehmen aufschreiben
fall through	fracasar	échouer	durchfallen
fall behind	atrasarse	être en retard, en arrière	zurück bleiben
give in	darse por, vencido, rendirse	se rendre à	nachgeben

English	Spanish	French	German
give off	producir, despedir	produire, exhaler	abgeben
give out	repartir, acabarse	distribuer, être épuisé	ausgeben, verteilen
have it in for	tenérselas juradas a uno, tenerla cogida con uno	en vouloir à quelqu'un	Abneigung haben
have it out with	poner las cosas en claro, ventilar un asunto con alguien	régler quelque chose	ausfechten
hold off	aguantar, aplazar	cesser, s'arrêter, retenir, retarder	anhalten andauern
hold out	resistir, durar	durer, être suffisant, résister	aushalten ausreichen
hold over	mantener, posponer	continuer à montrer	verlegen

Lesson 28

English	Spanish	French	German
let up	disminuir aflojar, relajar	diminuer, relâcher	nachlassen
lay off	parar, dejar cesante, despedir	arrêter, mettre au chômage	anhalten, entlassen, ablegen
bring out	sacar, presentar	présenter, faire paraître	hervorbringen
bring back	devolver	rapporter	zurückbringen
wait up for	esperar por, desvelarse en espera de	attendre	auf jemanden warten
leave alone	dejar tranquilo	laisser tranquille	alleine lassen
let alone	sin mencionar	encore moins	geschweige denn
break off	terminar, finalizar	rompre avec	abbrechen

wear off	pasar, desaparecer	disparaître (peu à peu)	verschwinden, aufhören
wear down	gastar	user complètement	abreten, abnützen, ausnützen
on the whole	en general	en somme, à tour prendre	im Allge- meinen
touch and go	arriesgado	l'issue est restée incertaine jusqu'au bout	riskant

Lesson 29

work out	hacer ejercicio, planear, resultar	exercer, e' la borer (Élaborer)	Bewegung machen, kunstroll
back up	dar marcha atrás defender	faire marche arrière, défendre	zurücksetzen, verteidigen
back out	salir, retirarse, decidir lo contrario	sortir, changer d'avis	die Meinung ändern, sich zurückziehen
have one's heart set on	anhelar, ansiar	avoir envie de tenir à	Wunsch haben
buy up	adquirir, acaparar	faire l'achat total	aufkaufen
buy out	comprar la parte de	acheter la part de	auszahlen, ankaufen
sell out	vender, liquidar	liquider	ausverkaufen
catch on	popularizarse, darse cuenta, entender	devenir populaire y être, comprendre	volkstümlich machen, verstehen, begreifen
be cut out for	tener talento para	avoir l'étoffe de	veranlagt sein
throw out	echar, botar	jeter à la porte, rejeter	herauswerfen, wegwerfen

English	Spanish	French	German
throw up	erigir, vomitar	ériger, vomir	errichten, sie übergeben
clear up	aclarar, solucionar	s'éclaircir clarifier, résoudre	auferlären

Lesson 30

slow down	ir más despacio	ralentir	langsamer werden
dry up	secarse completamente	sécher	austrocknen
dry out	secarse poco a poco	dessécher	autrocknen
be up to (something)	tener algo entre manos	machiner, combiner	planen, beabsichtigen, vorhaben
beat around the bush	andarse con rodeos	tourner autour du pot	indirekt sprechen
come to an end	terminar, acabarse	se terminer	beenden, zum Ende bringen
put an end to	darle fin a	faire cesser quelque chose	Schluss machen
get even with	vengarse	se venger	sich revanchieren
fool around	perder el tiempo, bromear	perdre son temps	Unsinn machen
look out on	dar a	donner sur	Aussicht haben auf
stir up	provocar, incitar	exciter, pousser à, agiter	aufhetzen
take in	escuchar, engañar	voir, décevoir	besuchen, betrügen

Lesson 31

go through	sufrir, consumir,	souffrir, consumer	durchamachen verzehren
go without saying	estar sobre-entendido	il va sans dire que	ohne Zweifel

put (someone) on	bromear	faire marcher quelqu'un	hintergehen
keep one's head	mantener la calma	garder son sang froid	den Kopf behalten
lose one's head	perder la cabeza	perdre la tête	den Kopf verlieren
narrow-minded	de mirar estrechas	à l'esprit étroit	engherzig
stand up	durar, dejar plantado	faire bon usage, résister, poser un lapin	halten, aufsitzen lassen
get the better of	aventajar	l'emporter sur	Überhand gewinnen
break loose	soltarse, zafarse	se détacher de, s'échapper, s'évader	losbrechen, ausbrechen
on edge	ansioso, irritable	énerver	aufgergt sein
waste one's breath	perder el tiempo	perdre son temps	Wörter ohne Ergebnis verschwenden
cut short	adelantar, reducir	couper court	abschneiden, abkurtzen

Lesson 32

step in	intervenir, entrar	intervenir, entrer	einschreiten, eintreten
step down	retirarse, renunciar	démissionner	eine Stellung aufgeben
step on	regañar, apurarse	reprimander, se dépêcher	einschreiten, sichbieilen
a steal	una ganga	une occasion	beilling sein
play up to	dar coba, adular	flatter	jemanden schmeicheln
more or less	casi, más o menos	presque, plus ou moins	mehr oder weniger
screw up	echar a perder confundir	ruiner, gâter	durcheinanderbringen

English	Spanish	French	German
goof up	pifiar, fallar	faire une gaffe	einen Fehler machen
go off the deep end	montar en cólera y hacer algo precipitadamente	e'emporter, s'emballer	etwas ohne Achtung machen
lose one's touch	perder la maña	perdre la main ou la touche	seine Geschick-lichkeit
in hand	bajo control	au poing	im Griff haben
on hand	a mano	à portée de la main	verfübar

Lesson 33

English	Spanish	French	German
kick (some-thing) around	debatir un asunto	ruminer, desculir	etwas überdenken, überlegen
on the ball	alerta, listo	alerte	auf draht sein
make up	compensar, inventar, maquillarse	se ratrapper, inventer se maquiller	gutmachen erfinden zurecht machen (Angesicht)
make up with	reconciliarse	se réconcilier	sich (wieder) versöhnen
pull together	calmarse	rassambler, se calmer	sich zusammen-reissen
be looking up	estar mejorando	être à la hausee, s'améliorer	besser werden
kick the habit	dejar un vicio	se débarasser du vice	eine schlechte Angewohnheit aufgeben
cover up	encubrir	dissimuler	verdecken
drop off	dormirse, entregar, bajar rápido	s'endormir livrer, tomber rapidement	einschlafen, befreien, abfallen

turn over	poner al revés, transferir	reverser, transférer	umkehren, weitergeben
go through channels	hacer algo debidamente	aller par entremise ou par voies	durch Mitteln gehen
last straw	el colmo	le comble	zuviel des Guten

Lesson 34

get cold feet	acobardarse, rajarse	avoir la frousse	verunsichert werden
trade in	canjear, cambiar	échanger	umstauschen
face to face	cara a cara	face à face	von Angesicht zu Angesecht
be with (someone)	estar de parte de, acordar	être avec quelqu'un	jemanden verstehen
be with it	estar alerta, en forma	se mettre à la mode	ganz dabei sein
fall for	enamorarse, tragárselo, caer en la trampa	tomber amoureux de, se laisser prendre a	Liebe auf dem ersten Blick empfinden, hereinfallen auf
it figures	por supuesto, claro	c'est logique ou normal	es ist möglich
fill (someone) in	informar, orientar	mettre au courant	benachreichtigen
make (someone) tick	motivar a	motiver, pousser	was jemanden bewegt
cover for	asumir los deberes de otra persona	couvrir, remplacer	fur jemand anderes einstehen
give (someone) a break	darle oportunidad- a alguien	donner une chance ou une opportunité	jemanden eine Chance geben
bow out	salirse	démissionner	aufgeben

English	Spanish	French	German
Lesson 35			
pin on	responsabilizar	accuser, jeter la faute sur quelqu'un	jemanden die Schuld fur etwas geben
get a rise out of	causar enojo a alguien	mettre en colère	sich uber jemanden amüsieren
stick around	quedarse en el mismo sitio	ne pas quitter, demeurer	herumlungern
pick up the tab	pagar la cuenta	financer, régler la facture	die Rechnung bezahlen
by the way	de paso, incidentalmente	à propos	im Vorübergehen
go to town	excederse	exagérer	etwas grundlich machen
let slide	evitar una responsabilidad	négliger, laisser aller les choses	etwas vernäch-lassigen
search me	¡Que a mí no me pregunten!	ne pas avoir la moindre idée	ich weiss es nicht
get off one's chest	desahogarse	déballer	von der Seele schaffen
live it up	darse vida de rico	mener la belle vie	hoch leben
liven up	animar	égayer	munter werden
have a voice in	tener voz en algun asúnto	avoir une voix au chapitre	etwas zu zagen haben
Lesson 36			
check in	llegar a un hotel	s'inscrire sur le registre d'un hotel	einchecken

check out	pagar la cuenta de un hotel	régler son compte en quitant un hôtel	abrechnen, untersuchen
take at one's word	creer incondicionalmente	prendre quelqu'un au mot	glaubwürdig sein
serve one's purpose	ser de utilidad, convenirle a	faire l'affaire	behilfich sein
in the worst way	sobremanera, en alto grado	à tout prix, désespérément	sehr, um alles
cop out	evadir una responsabilidad	renoncer à, eviter ses responsabilités	zurückziehen
line up	preparar algo o alguien	s'aligner, préparer	besorgen
lose one's cool	perder la calma	perdre son sang-froid	sich aufregen
leave open	dejar pendiente	laisser en suspens	etwas verschieben
turn on	excitarlo a uno, entusiasmarlo	exciter, inspirer	grosse Interesse in etwas haben
miss the boat	perder una oportunidad	rater l'opportunité	eine Gelegenheit ver passen
think up	inventar	inventer	aufdenken

Lesson 37

throw (someone) a curve	confundir, cogerlo a uno desprevenido	confondre	jemanden in irreführen
make waves	romper la calma, estorbar el orden	faire des histoires	etwas ausser Fassung bringen
carry on	continuar	continuer	weitermachen
not on your life	ni hablar de eso	jamais de la vie	überhaupt nicht, nie

English	Spanish	French	German
cover ground	llevar mucho a cabo	couvrir beaucoup de terrain	sehr umfassend sein
mind the store	cuidar de algo, ocuparse del negocio	surveiller la boutique	auf etwas Acht geben
throw the book at	castigar severamente	être strict ou dur	sehr streng sein
put one's foot in	meter la pata	mettre le pied dans le plat	sich blamieren
be up for grabs	estar disponible, fácil de obtener	être disponible	zum Verkauf geben sein
show off	jactarse	faire parade de	eingebildet sein
learn the ropes	aprender las rutinas	aprendre son affaire	sicheinleben
keep one's fingers crossed	ojalá que así sea	avoir bon espoir	Glück haben

Lesson 38

English	Spanish	French	German
land on one's feet	caer de pie como un gato	tomber à quatres pattes	sich unversehrt
dish out	dar algo en abundancia, derrochar, dar a manos llenas	servir, critiquer	jemanden kritisieren
get through to	hacer entender a alguien	s'entendre avec	jemanden verstehen
keep one's word	cumplir lo prometido	tenir sa parolé	Kersprechung-halten
be over one's head	estar abrumado	être accable	zuviel sein
ask for	merecer algún castigo o contrariedad	mériter une punition adversité	verdienen sich verdient machen
be a far cry from	ser muy distinto	être trés différent	sehr verschieden

by all means	definitivamente	bien sûr	selbstverständ-lich
get out from under	salir a flote	surmonter ses pertes	sich finan-ziell erholen
take the bull by the horns	enfrentarse con	être déterminé, décisif	etwas mit Bestimmung
give (someone) a hand	echar una mano	donner un coup de mains	jemanden behilflich sein
give (someone) a big hand	aplaudir efusivamente	applaudir fortement	Beifall spenden

Lesson 39

goof off	vaguear	être oisif	faulenzen
talk back to	protestar	rétorquer	dagegenreden
be in	estar a la moda	être à la page	modern sein
be out	estar fuera de moda	hors de mode	altmodisch setzen
draw the line at	definir el límite en	se refuser à	Grenzen setzen
get out of line	desobedecer	désobéir	Grenzen über-schreiten
dry run	ensayo	faire des essais ou des épreuves	eine Probe
play by ear	tocar algo de oído	jouer par oreille	ein Stück Musik auswending
be in (someone's) shoes	estar en la posición de otro	être à la place d'autre	nachempfinden
keep after	recordar constantemente	rappeler continûement, harceler	dran bleiben
fix up	arreglar concertar una cita	réparer, assigner un rendezvous	etwas aufsetzen für jemanden
be had	ser engañado, timado, estafado	être roulé, trompé, dupé, volé	beschwindelt